Our Townlet Swir
(Svir, Belarus)

Translation of
Ayaratenu Swir

Original Book Edited by: Dr. Chanoch Swironi (Drutz)

Originally published in Tel Aviv 1959

A Publication of JewishGen
Edmond J. Safra Plaza, 36 Battery Place, New York, NY 10280
646.494.2972 | info@JewishGen.org | www.jewishgen.org

©JewishGen 2024. All Rights Reserved.
JewishGen is the Genealogical Research Division of the
Museum of Jewish Heritage – A Living Memorial to the Holocaust

Our Townlet Swir
Translation of *Ayaratenu Swir*

Copyright © 2024 by JewishGen. All rights reserved.
First Printing: July 2024, Tammuz, 5784
Editor of Original Yizkor Book: Dr. Chanoch Swironi (Drutz)
Translation Project Coordinator: Lee Harrison z"l
Cover Design: Irv Osterer
Layout: Jonathan Wind
Name Indexing: Stefanie Holzman

This book may not be reproduced, in whole or in part, including illustrations in any form (beyond that copying permitted by Sections 107 and 108 of the U.S. Copyright Law and except by reviewers for public press), without written permission from the publisher.

JewishGen Press is not responsible for inaccuracies or omissions in the original work and makes no representations regarding the accuracy of this translation. Digital images of the original book's contents can be seen online at the New York Public Library website or the Yiddish Book Center website.

Library of Congress Control Number (LCCN): 2024939766

ISBN: 978-1-962054-01-0 (hard cover: 210 pages, alk. paper)

About JewishGen.org

JewishGen, is a Genealogical Research Division of the Museum of Jewish Heritage - A Living Memorial to the Holocaust, serves as the global home for Jewish genealogy.

Featuring unparalleled access to 30+ million records, it offers unique search tools, along with opportunities for researchers to connect with others who share similar interests. Award winning resources such as the Family Finder, Discussion Groups, and ViewMate, are relied upon by thousands each day.

In addition, JewishGen's extensive informational, educational and historical offerings, such as the Jewish Communities Database, Yizkor Book translations, InfoFiles, Family Tree of the Jewish People, and KehilaLinks, provide critical insights, first-hand accounts, and context about Jewish communal and familial life throughout the world.

Offered as a free resource, JewishGen.org has facilitated thousands of family connections and success stories, and is currently engaged in an intensive expansion effort that will bring many more records, tools, and resources to its collections.

Please visit https://www.jewishgen.org/ to learn more.

Executive Director: Avraham Groll

About the JewishGen Yizkor Book Project

Yizkor Books (Memorial Books) were traditionally written to memorialize the names of departed family and martyrs during holiday services in the synagogue (a practice that still exists in many synagogues today).

Over the centuries, as a result of countless persecutions and horrific atrocities committed against the Jews, Yizkor Books (Sefer Zikaron in Hebrew) were expanded to include more historical information, such as biographical sketches of famous personalities and descriptions of daily town life.

Following the Holocaust, the idea of remembrance and learning took on an urgent and crucial importance. Survivors of the Holocaust sought out other surviving residents of their former towns to memorialize and document the names and way of life of those who were ruthlessly murdered by the Nazis. These remembrances were documented in Yizkor Books, hundreds of which were published in the first decades after the Holocaust.

Most of these books were published privately, or through *Landsmanshaftn* (social organizations comprised of members originating from the same European town or region) that still existed, and were often distributed free of charge. The languages used to document these crucial histories and links to our past were Yiddish and Hebrew. JewishGen has undertaken the sacred responsibility of translating these books into English so that the culture and way of life of these communities will be preserved and transmitted to future generations.

In 1986, a group of farsighted JewishGenners started a project to pool their efforts together in groups based upon their ancestors' towns and donate funds to translate the Yizkor books of their ancestral towns into English. As the translated material became available, it was made accessible for free at https://www.JewishGen.org/Yizkor . Hardcover copies can be purchased by visiting https://www.jewishgen.org/Yizkor/ybip.html (see below).

It is our hope that the translation of these books into English (and other languages) will assist the countless Jewish family researchers who are so desperately seeking to forge a connection with their heritage.

Director of JewishGen Yizkor Book Project: Lance Ackerfeld

About JewishGen Press

JewishGen Press (formerly the Yizkor Books-in-Print Project) is the publishing division of JewishGen.org, and provides a venue for the publication of non-fiction books pertaining to Jewish genealogy, history, culture, and heritage.

In addition to the Yizkor Book category, publications in the Other Non-Fiction category include Shoah memoirs and research, genealogical research, collections of genealogical and historical materials, biographies, diaries and letters, studies of Jewish experience and cultural life in the past, academic theses, and other books of interest to the Jewish community.

Please visit https://www.jewishgen.org/Yizkor/ybip.html to learn more.

Director of JewishGen Press: Joel Alpert
Managing Editor - Jessica Feinstein
Publications Manager - Susan Rosin

Notes to the Reader

The images in the original book were reproduced from photographs from the time of the first edition. These reproductions were already of poor quality, being pre-war and at least 30 or more years old. As a result, the images in the book are the best achievable.

A reader can view the original scans of the book on the websites listed below.

The original book can be seen online at the Yiddish Book Center website:

https://www.yiddishbookcenter.org/collections/yizkor-books/yzk-nybc314031/swironi-chanoch-unzer-shtetele-svir

OR

at the New York Public Library Digital Collections website:

https://digitalcollections.nypl.org/items/f34018b0-3569-0133-b73c-00505686a51c

To obtain a list of Shoah victims from **Swir (Svir, Belarus),** the reader should access the Yad Vashem web site listed below; one can also search for specific family names using family name option. These lists are continually updated by Yad Vashem, so it is worthwhile to periodically search these lists.

There is more valuable information (including the Pages of Testimony, etc.) available on this website: https://yvng.yadvashem.org/

A list of all books available from JewishGen Press along with prices is available at: https://www.jewishgen.org/Yizkor/ybip.html

Additional resources for Svir are:

https://kehilalinks.jewishgen.org/Svir/

Cover Photo Credits

Cover Design by: Irv Osterer

Front Cover:
The Synagogue in Svir [Page 35]

Back Cover:
Top Left: Henekh Miller and Malke Fisher [Page 77]
Top Right: Svir He'khalutz group in 1931
Middle: Map showing location of Svir – Irv Osterer
Bottom: Velvl the Blacksmith [Page 103]

Swir Geopolitical Information

Svir, Belarus is located at 54°51' N 26°24' E and 81 miles NW of Minsk

	Town	District	Province	Country
Before WWI (c. 1900):	Svir	Sventsyany	Vilna	Russian Empire
Between the wars (c. 1930):	Świr	Święciany	Wilno	Poland
After WWII (c. 1950):	Svir'			Soviet Union
Today (c. 2000):	Śvir			Belarus

Alternate Names for the Town:

Svir' [Rus], Świr [Pol], Śvir [Bel], Svir [Yid], Svieriai [Lith], Svyriai, Shvir

Nearby Jewish Communities:

Mikhalishki 10 miles WSW
Narach 13 miles ENE
Lyntupy 14 miles NNW
Vornyany 17 miles WSW
Kamelishki 21 miles W
Bystrytsa 21 miles W
Myadzyel 21 miles E
Adutiškis, Lithuania 22 miles NNE
Švenčionys, Lithuania 23 miles NNW
Stajetiškė, Lithuania 23 miles N
Astravyets 24 miles SW
Soly 25 miles SSW
Pastavy 25 miles NE
Smarhon 25 miles S
Pabradė, Lithuania 27 miles WNW
Švenčionėliai, Lithuania 27 miles NW
Mielagėnai, Lithuania 28 miles N
Ceikiniai, Lithuania 29 miles N
Zhuprany 29 miles SSW
Kurenets 30 miles SE

Jewish Population: 1,114 (in 1897), 820 (in 1925)

Map of Belarus showing the location of Svir

Table of Contents

Translated by Gloria Berkenstat Freund

Introduction

Upon the Publication of the Book	Dov Joel	3
A Book - A Monument	Heshl Miller	4
These things I remember, and pour out my soul within me	Shmuel Dobkin	5
The Town of Svir	Dr. Chanoch Swironi	6
To the offspring of former residents of Svir	Dov Joel	7
Upon the Publication of the Book	Dov Joel	8

Chapter One
The Historic Development and Geographic Situation

Our Small Shtetele [Town]	Chanoch Drutz	11
Highlights of the History of Svir	Herzl Weiner	12
The Geographic and Economic Situation	Berl Alperovitz	14
General Appearance	Herzl Weiner	15
The River	Herzl Weiner	16
The Bridge	Herzl Weiner	17
Svirer Life According to the Vilner Pinkes, YEKOPO		18

Chapter Two
The Cultural and Social Life

A Cultural and Social Shtetele	Chanoch Drutz	21
The People's Library	Herzl Weiner	31
The First Elementary School in Svir	Shmuel Dobkin	33
The first Hebrew School in Svir	Chaim Rugovin	34
The Svir Gymnastics and Sports Club	Berl Alperovitz	41
The Svir Jewish Defense	Dr. Ch. Swironi	47
The Svir Journals	Herzl Weiner	48

Chapter Three
Terrible Cases of Misfortune

Avremele Yoel	Chanoch Drutz	60
Misfortune in the Hachshara [training for pioneers to Eretz-Yisroel]	Dr. Ch. Swironi	65

Chapter Four
Memories

Memories of a Kheder-Yingl [religious primary school boy]	Aharon Koury	70
Toiling Jews	Matityahu Bogdanov	71
Memories of Svir	Ben-Tzion Gold	73
Remembrances of Svir	Joe Salav	77
My Birthplace	Shoshana Drapkin	78
From the days of my childhood	Arye Gur-Arye (Pekel)	80

Chapter Five
The Destruction of Svir

Memorial Candle	Shmuel Dobkin	84
Destruction and Revenge Poems	Fanya Fisher	85
Last Letters	Shlomo and Yitzhak Rabinovits	90
The Demise of Svir	Dr. Chanoch Swironi	91
Memories of an Eyewitness	Tsivye Dobkin	100
A Svir Partisan	Chanoch Drutz	105
Christian Angels	Dr. Chanoch Swironi	111
From the Poem: In the City of Slaughter	Haim Nachman Bialik	123
Svir After Hitler's Downfall	Chanoch Drutz	123
El Male Rahamim		126
List of the Martyrs from the community of Svir		127

Chapter Six
The Svirer in America and Other Lands

Svirer Social and Aid Association in America		147
List of Active Members of the Svir Organization in New York	Matityahu Bogdanov, Avraham Chayat, Melekh Levin and Aharon Koury	150
List of Former Residents of Svir in America		153
List of Former Svir Residents in Other Countries		156

Chapter Seven
The Svirer in the Land of Israel

At the Annual Svir Gathering	Shmuel Dobkin	160
The Svir Immigrants in Israel, their Association and their Interest-Free Fund	Dov Joel	162
The Svirer in Eretz-Yisroel	Dr. Chanoch Swironi	173
A memorial prayer for former residents of Svir		182
List of the Svirer Jews in the Land of Israel		183

Name Index of English Edition 188

Our Townlet Swir
(Svir, Belarus)

54°51' / 26°24'

Translation of
Ayaratenu Swir

Editor: Dr. Chanoch Swironi (Drutz)

Published in Tel Aviv 1959

Acknowledgments:

Project Coordinator

Lee Harrison z"l

Our sincere appreciation to Zev Swironi, son of Dr. Chanoch Swironi (Drutz) z"l, for permission to put this material on the JewishGen web site.

Our sincere appreciation to Yad Vashem for the submission of the necrology for placement on the JewishGen web site.

This is a translation of: *Ayaratenu Swir* (Our Townlet Swir),
Editor: Dr. Chanoch Swironi (Drutz), Former Residents of Swir in Israel and in the United States,
Published: Tel Aviv 1959 (H,Y 240 pages)

Note: The original book can be seen online at the NY Public Library site: Svir (1959)

This material is made available by JewishGen, Inc. and the Yizkor Book Project for the purpose of fulfilling our mission of disseminating information about the Holocaust and destroyed Jewish communities.
This material may not be copied, sold or bartered without JewishGen, Inc.'s permission. Rights may be reserved by the copyright holder.

JewishGen, Inc. makes no representations regarding the accuracy of the translation. The reader may wish to refer to the original material for verification.
JewishGen is not responsible for inaccuracies or omissions in the original work and cannot rewrite or edit the text to correct inaccuracies and/or omissions.
Our mission is to produce a translation of the original work and we cannot verify the accuracy of statements or alter facts cited.

OUR TOWNLET
SWIR

Edited by
Dr CHANOCH SWIRONI (DRUTZ)

Published by the "Irgun Yozei Swir in Israel" with the assistance of the "Swirer Social and Help Society in the United States."

Printed in Israel 1959

[Page 5- Hebrew] [Page 11 - Yiddish]

Upon the Publication of the Book

by Dov Joel

Translated by Mindle Crystel Gross

Edited by Toby Bird z"l

This book, "Our Town Svir", will immortalize our birthplace, her Jewish past, her social and cultural life and will erect a monument to the martyrs who were murdered, who perished at the hands of the Hitler bandits during the Second World War.

This book is written in Yiddish so that it can be read by all from Svir who, regretfully, do not know the Hebrew language because they are spread throughout the entire world.

Preparing a book such as this for publication took many years. The bulk of the material had already been completed about ten years ago, but we decided to wait and gather more material.

However it turned out that we received too much material, and we did not have the financial means to print all of it.

As a result, this book contains no more than one-third of the submitted material.

This book incorporates a number of articles and descriptions written in different ways.

1. "The Little Town of Svir" by Dr. Chanoch Drutz, which, in the original, consisted of 260 printed pages.
2. Articles by Herzl Weiner, Sarah Nakhum, which consisted of approximately 100 pages. He is known as an author whose poems have been published in various newspapers.
3. Memories and descriptions of Berl Alperovitz, Paris, consisting of approximately more than 50 pages.
4. The book by Fonye Fisher which consists of 120 pages.

He expresses the pain and sorrow of a woman from Svir who escaped from Hitler's bandits, but who lost her husband and children.

Because of financial reasons, we decided to print only a portion of this colossal material.

In order to select the material, we elected a group of editors – colleagues from the following friends:

Dr. Chanoch Swironi, 2) Hershl Miller, 3) Gershon Yael, 5) Shmuel Dobkin, 5) Hertsl Weiner

Chief editor was Dr. Chanoch Swironi (Drutz)

In addition, the decision was made to print a complete list of all the martyrs of Svir in alphabetical order.

In conclusion, I fulfill my debt by sending a hearty thank you to all the friends who helped in the publication of this book, both those who live with us in the State of Israel and those who are elsewhere in the world, most especially in the United States of America.

[Page 6 - Hebrew] [Page 12 - Yiddish]

A Book – a Monument

by Heshl Miller

Translated by Mindle Crystel Gross

Edited by Toby Bird z"l

Now, at this time of the publication of our Yizkor book, it is worthwhile to note the responsibility we all feel to the memory of our holy martyrs with the placing for them of a monument in the form of a book.

This book will remind our generation and future generations of the little town of Svir and her Jewish community which was ripped out by its roots and of which no remnant remains.

All our nearest and dearest who perished in such a barbaric fashion are mentioned in this book with the greatest heartfelt pain and rivers of tears spilled by those remaining from Svir around the world.

Therefore, it is understandable that all those from Svir who find themselves here in the State of Israel did not rest, and despite all difficulties, decided to publish this Yizkor book.

Each one of us is responsible to his children to relate the contents of this book and to tell them about the horrific destruction of the old home. We here must do everything so that our slaughtered families are not forgotten.

All will be able to read in this book the tragic history of the destruction of Svir, a beautiful Jewish community which disappeared in blood and flames.

[Page 7]

These things I remember, and pour out my soul within me

(The Book of Psalms 42:4)

Shmuel Dobkin

Translated by Sara Mages

With awe and compassion we publish the memorial book for the community of Svir which was destroyed.

Almost seventeen years have passed since that bitter and impetuous day in which our parents, brothers, sisters and loved ones, were destroyed in all kinds of unnatural cruel deaths.

The farther we move away from the day of disaster, the more we feel the bereavement and the void that was created in the world of each one of us. And even if our Sages of blessed memory said (Blessings page 58): "The dead is only forgotten from the heart after twelve months", these words are only related to one mourning, but not for such a terrible Holocaust that destroyed millions of our brothers. And for that reason, the wound is deep and bleeding. Our soul will cry in secret and there is no consolation. The blood of our loved ones is crying out to us from the Valley of Death, demanding of us to reward them with a last loving grace, and it is: to establish a monument in their sacred memory so we won't forget them, and for the future generations, so they'll know the pure and innocent martyrs who were destroyed. After many deliberations and efforts, we were able to establish this memorial project in the form of a memorial book for our community, the holy community of Svir.

This book will fold in it the scroll of the beginnings and the aftermath of our town. It will tell us, and generations to come, about the vibrant life of our town, in all areas and periods. About its glory and sufferings, rise and fall, joy and grief, and the community's last days – about its destruction. And the beloved images of our parents and loved ones, who perished somewhere in the Vale of Tears, will hover before our eyes. We will read this book in moments of memory and communion, lend an ear, feel that we breathe their breath, and hear their voices, thoughts and conversations. Then, the heart will sight and the soul will be shocked because an entire world was destroyed, and our lips will whisper: These things I remember, and pour out my soul within me!

[Page 8]

The Town of Svir

Dr. Chanoch Swironi

Translated by Sara Mages

A.

The town of Svir is located about 80 Kilometers from Vilna, the capital of Lita, in the Švenčionys district. Its closest neighboring towns are: Kabilnik, Mikhalishak, Sventzyen, Lintupis, Adutiškis, Oshmiana, Postavy and Smarhon.

The town lay by a rather large lake, from which a stream flowed to the Viliya River, a tributary of the Nimen River. At the outskirts of town, a wooden bridge crossed the river and served as the main gateway to the town. A mound, which was known in the area by the name: the "Svir Mountain", rose in the center. Napoleon built on it an important military position during his march to Russia. The town was established at the end of the 18th century, and a few Jewish families are mentioned in a government's document from 1770. After the expulsion of Jews from the villages, the settlement started to grow and develop. Before the First World War, the Jewish community numbered approximately 200 families, 1100 persons.

A great fire broke out in town at the end of the 19th century, and almost all the houses went up in flames. The town's residents quickly raised its ruins and re-built it.

Most of the Jews engaged in retail trade. Only a few merchants rose to the rank of wholesalers. Only several dozen families made their living from farming and labor.

B.

Svir wasn't a large Jewish community, but a vibrant colorful cultural and social life pulsed in it. The Jewish elementary school, which was founded by *"Tarbut"*, stood on a significant educational level.

The youth organizations, which were affiliated with the Israeli labor movement: *"HeHalutz"*, *"HeHalutz Hatzair"* and *"Hashomer Hatzair"*, teemed with life and gathered around them almost all the Jewish youth.

There were magnificent public institutions for mutual aid in town: *"Mishmeret Cholim"* [sick fund], *"Gemilut Chesed"* [acts of loving kindness] and a "Jewish National Bank".

[Page 9]

The youth invested a lot of thought and energy in the "Drama Club", which managed to produce a number of elaborate plays. The wind instruments band, which was established by the "Volunteer irefighters Association", served as a superb cultural tool and contributed to the success of various public appearances. Various divisions were operated by the sports organizations (*"Maccabi"* and *"Hapoel"*), and the soccer teams acquired a good name.

The public library consisted of about 3,000 books from the best of Hebrew, Yiddish and world literature.

In general, the Jewish population stood at an adequate cultural level. Almost every Jewish home read a daily newspaper that was published in Warsaw or Vilna.

Due to lack of means, two or three families have signed for one newspaper. Everyone wanted to know what was happening in the world and in Israel. When a lecturer came to town, he always found an alert audience.

The older generation sat every evening in Beit Hamidrash and listened to the daily Gemara page.

In short, all the social circles were thirsty for knowledge and driven for education. Many parents went hungry in order to send their children to study in the capital city of Vilna.

All the former residents of Svir, wherever they are, in Israel, Europe and America, are attached to the cradle of their childhood with their heart and soul, and remember it with love, quiver, anxiety and love.

With the destruction of the community of Svir during the terrible Holocaust, which all the European Jewry experienced during the Second World War, a pure Jewish spring dried up and a good Jewish heart stopped beating. A cultural nest, in which our parents, brothers and sisters, the honest and the innocent, working people, dedicated and loyal to the Jewish nation and the country of Israel, was destroyed.

May our sons and daughters keep the memory of the martyrs of Svir's community in their hearts forever, and like us, they will remember it with love and gratitude.

This will be our consolation in our deep grief over the loss of our precious loved ones.

[Page 10]

To the offspring of former residents of Svir

Dov Joel

Translated by Sara Mages

This book "Our Little Town of Svir" describes the lives of the Jews in the town of Svir – the birthplace of your parents.

The book is written in "Yiddish" – their childhood language, which you don't speak and for sure you can't read in a book. You grew up under different circumstances than your parents, and maybe you know very little about Jewish life in towns in Poland and Russia, a generation or two ago.

But perhaps, when this book will arrive to your home, you'll want to know what's written in it, and maybe you'll be interested to hear something about your parents' childhood place.

The Hebrew article of Dr. Chanoch Swironi (Drutz), the editor of this book, describes the town of "Svir" in the most general terms.

For sure you know that many Jewish communities were destroyed in the Second World War by German soldiers, that the Jewish nation lost 6 million sons and daughters, and we, the survivors of these communities, must always remembers the members of our nation that we lost. We hope that you want to know about the past life of the Jewish nation, and that you will also keep in touch with the present and future of the Jewish nation.

[Page 13]

A Book About Svir

by Aaron Koury, New York

Translated by Mindle Crystel Gross

Edited by Toby Bird z"l

The book, "Our Little Town of Svir" is nicely presented and a sincere "Thank You: is due our friend, Dr. Drutz, for the time and effort which he invested in it.

Having left Svir so many years ago and leaving it in a state of filth in which Jews lived, because life must be lived without questioning it, where there was no place to spend a pleasant hour - being away from Svir for so many years, and returning from larger cities, a youth such as I who had to spend some time in Svir felt the stifling atmosphere in the life of the town. That is why, reading this book, a newly-born Svir opened up before me, a town where one could enter a library and a club, discuss, delve into a single purpose, see a theatre performance, skate with real skates on the lake, ride a bicycle, hear Svir trumpets in a quartet. This was as fresh water for me who was in the desert. I was astonished when I read all of this in the book.

I want to remember the difference between my time in Svir and the time which is described in the book.

When our boys wanted to skate on the lake, they had to hide so that the fathers would not know because it was not seemly for Jewish boys to think about such foolishness. Swimming was so difficult and so seldom that a Jewish boy could not learn to swim. He was always reminded that he was not a "sheygets" (non-Jewish boy), that he must have in mind his future.

When I was in Svir the last time, many, many years ago, I was already quite a grown-up youth. Bentchl Zlatayobke and I agreed to go fishing. We made a fine rod with a string of real horsehair and worked it all out at the mill. We sat at the water, talked about various worldly topics which Bentchl solved, and the rod stood hidden in the water for hours and did not catch a fish. Each day we hid the rod for the next day or the day after that, Each time no fish was caught even though our rod was in the water. We were still pleased with our fishing and our secret because if the Jews of Svir would have known we would have really been severely punished. We most certainly would have gotten the nickname of "Fisher" or "Fish-catcher." We decided once that if, G-d forbid, we were caught with the pole, we would buy a few fish from a Christian and march into the lake with them to demonstrate that we knew how to do this. But we were very afraid of what they would do to us, and we were thrilled that nobody ever caught us near the mill. This is how it once was in Svir.

Now I read that Jewish boys rowed on Shabos, skated, played football and published a newspaper. Residents of Svir write poetry, act in the theatre. It is virtually unbelievable.

This book, for those from Svir who are scattered all over the world, revealed a new world, and it is pleasant for everyone to read that our beautiful old home had changed.

The horror is that this warm and beautiful home was so tragically destroyed.

Halutzim from Svir in Israel 1924

In this photo we find two halutzim: Chaim Chayat and Shoshana Chazan whose aliya took place before the big halutzim movement in Svir. Thanks to them, the Svir Jewish kibbutz in Eretz Israel has more than 100 members.

[Page 19]

Chapter One
The Historic Development and Geographic Situation

Our Small *Shtetele* [Town]

by Chanoch Drutz

Translated by Mindle Crystel Gross

Edited by Toby Bird z"l

The little town of Svir where we saw for the first time in our lives the rays of the sun, the little town where we heard childish voices for the first time, the little town where our first footsteps fell, the little town where we, during our childhood years, frolicked and played, is that little town, and is for everyone who had been born there, a part of his flesh and blood.

A long street, two market-squares, one at each end, with a few small streets, was all that comprised Svir, but nevertheless, she is to us, the children of Svir, much more, and more appealing than other little towns. There were almost no brick houses in Svir, only one, and the second floor was constructed of wood.

A street in the little town

The roofs were either shingled, tin or even straw. Many houses were already old during our time. There were houses that virtually had sunk into the ground right up to the windows. There were houses that did not have wooden floors. Very seldom was there a house in Svir with inside plumbing. In the main, water had to be carried from a distant well, and it is a wonder that nobody in that tiny village hated it. On the contrary, everyone was tied to Svir with his very being and life. In everyone we met, in New York, in Los Angeles, in Buenos Aires and in Cuba, in Paris and in Israel, in London and Tel-Aviv, there beat a single heart, there is one feeling everywhere. All are connected like brothers and sisters with their very lives and being, and all of this because of that tucked-away little corner in the vicinity of Vilna.

A stream flowed on one side and on the other side was a lake. This stream actually flowed from the lake close to the houses in town. All around there were forests, fields and villages. This town was not dipped in milk and honey, but in greenery and flowers, and as far as the eye could see, there were visible without end all kinds of fruit trees: apple, and pear, plum and cherry and blueberry bushes.

During the summer, the town was surrounded with ears of corn, oats, tall grass and wheat. During the winter, she was wrapped in a broad white sheet of snow.

And so the Jews of Svir lived a contented life. From the bridge to Dubeloner Street, lived good people in the old shacks, devoted friends, each of them. Everyone in his own house felt as a bird in the nest, until the wild barbarian arrived and destroyed the nest and its little birds.

Woe unto the destroyed, devoted birds of Svir, woe unto their shattered and burned nests.

[Page 21]

Highlights of the History of Svir

by Herzl Weiner

Translated by Mindle Crystel Gross

Edited by Toby Bird z"l

Unfortunately, we are missing much historical material and documentation which would have aided in describing the story of Svir. Not only was there not left any vestige of our little home-town which was torn out by its very roots, as well as the social and cultural life there, but we were also organically ripped from our origin and geographically isolated.

Today, the sources of information have dried up and we cannot find out any more about our faraway connection. The generation which would have enriched us with its knowledge has vanished, but yet, we are making the attempt to immortalize in short, modest sentences, her history.

It is clear that our little town carried the name of the famous Count Svirski whose dynasty, for hundreds of years, ruled over all of the surrounding area. It is told that at the very top of the mountain stood a very beautifully-built castle. Not only was the town named in his honor, but also many Jewish families of whom there were dozens in town bore the name of the great Count. Whether it was their choice or they were forced to do so is now difficult to determine with any degree of accuracy. Today's Svirsky families are spread throughout the world, descendants of our little town of Svir.

The Jewish community in Svir, according to all estimates, had existed for hundreds of years. The old cemetery bears witness to this, where there were sunk into the earth headstones which still had legible inscriptions and were 150 years old. The megila on which every death was recorded and the place of burial passed from one generation to the next and was a true historical document.

The majority of Jews in town had wandered in from the surrounding villages of nearby little towns. It is difficult to know today if this was due to their own free will or under pressure from the Tzarist government which had issued a law that Jews must leave the villages. Many-branched families carried the name of their village, as for example, the Pitsilekher, Shpiyaler, Duvnikirer, or of their town, such as the Kurnatkes, originated from the town of Kurenyetz, the Myadler, the Shwentzyaner, and so forth. The big fire which broke out at the end of the last century left almost no remnant of the town, and therefore, we do not have any old historical buildings and antiques.

The Road Up to the Mountain

The synagogue was rebuilt after the fire in the modern style. The town experienced numerous wars, and Napoleon and his army reached there. There is a legend that the Svir Mountain was created by him. The town emerged almost untouched from the First World War in 1914, because the front was several kilometers further away. Later, however, at the Polish-Bolshevik war in 1920, a battle was fought which involved the town. The invading Red Army found itself on the opposite side of the lake and among the retreating Polish army which established its stronghold on the mountain. The town was heavily bombed. A number of houses burned, and the entire Jewish population of the town moved to the cemetery. The next day, right after the Red Army marched in, they returned to their old homes. As it later became known, thanks to a coincidence, the entire Jewish population was saved, they who had hidden behind the trees in the cemetery. Suspicion by the Red Army fell upon the hateful Polish army. After all preparations had been completed to open fire with heavy artillery, the cry of a child was heard and the lowing of a cow. The distance was small and they were then convinced that there was only the civilian population there.

As those rescued later related, it was after the Second World War that the greatest portion of the town was destroyed. The synagogue was leveled to the ground. The entire area was covered over, and the neighboring Christians planted gardens there. Not a single reminder of a former Jewish life remained. But even more tragic, out of a total Jewish population of about 200 families, about 1,000 souls, only 100 were left alive, spread throughout the entire world, the majority of whom are to be found in Eretz Yisroel.

[Page 24]

The Geographic and Economic Situation

by Berl Alperovitz

Translated by Mindle Crystel Gross

Edited by Toby Bird z"l

Even at a distance of 5-6 km, we can see against the blue sky the contours of the town which stretch long and narrow. Most especially, we see the mountain – the Svir "Everest" and also the Svir skyscraper – the Judas tower.

Up until WWI, the train station closest to Svir was Lintufi, 24 km away. The German occupiers extended the train line to Constantinove.

Svir mountain and a partial street view

Svir is located in western White Russia. Svir's neighboring towns are: Kabilnik 20 km, Mikhalishak 21 km, Sventzyen 37 km, Smargan 42 km, Kurenitz 49 km.

Despite the fact that the town was located above sea level and was paved, it was very muddy on rainy days.

There were large swamps behind the town. The farmers from the other side of the lake would go through the mud, using it as a short-cut to town during the dry summer season, rolling up their pants high above the knees, splashing through. In the fall and spring, it was not possible to cross through the swamps. On the other sides of town, the ground was normal, tilled fields, meadows and a little pine forest, the so-called "Tushtser" forest.

Svir totaled approximately 1900 souls. Of these, 1100 were Jews and approximately 800 were non-Jews. A distinction must be made among the non-Jews – White Russian, Poles, Starovyern [old believers who had broken from the Russian Orthodox Church] and… one Tartar. Differentiating among the Christians - who was a White Russian, who was a Pole - was very difficult. The rich felt it beneath their honor to admit to being White Russian nationals. They struggle to speak Polish and say that they are Poles. Let us forgive them for this and regard those who spoke Polish as Poles.

The Jews occupied the "The Third of May Street" which stretched from the church to the horse- market, a distance of 1 km, that marked the boundaries of the town. A small number of Jews also lived on the side streets.

The Starovyern, a total of about several tens of families, lived in a little enclave on the side of town, along the edge of the lake. This village was called Slaboda.

Most of the Jewish population of Svir was merchants. At every house on the main street, there was a shop, shops of various kinds: fancy goods, groceries, hardware, bakeries, butchers and others. In many instances, these shops were not the only source of income. They were an additional source with which the women occupied themselves, as did their daughters. The men participated in trade. They dealt with everything – some in grain on a large scale. They would buy it up at the market and transport entire wagons to Vilna. Others traded in the same manner with potatoes, fruit, poultry, eggs, pelts, pig hair, and so forth. Naturally, not all of these merchants had many full wagons and not all of these merchants were simultaneously shopkeepers. There were also seasonal merchants, e.g., orchards.

There were also many Jews who were peddlers and craftsmen. The only help in their difficult battle for life that the Jews of Svir received was from the folk-bank and from the loan institution. According to a report from the Vilna Yekopa, there were more than 140 Svir residents enrolled as members.

The greatest portion of the Svir Jewish population lived modestly, not on a particularly wealthy level, but they were all satisfied and pleased, until WWII erupted and destroyed their impoverished life.

[Page 27]

General Appearance

by Herzl Weiner

Translated by Mindle Crystel Gross

Edited by Toby Bird z"l

Svir had her own specific appearance and was built differently from neighboring towns which was influenced by her special topographic situation. There were no flat plains, but downward slopes and valleys which led down to the broad flowing river. The mountain in the middle of the town was a pretty artistic corner in the so-called Vilna landscape. This attracted many artists from afar who immortalized the beauty of nature and the surroundings with their brushes.

Just past the bridge at the beginning of the town was the church, the priest's orchard and the surrounding little Christian houses, peasant huts. From the grain-market, the opposite side was also built up with peasant huts covered in straw. There began the street which sliced through the entire town up to the horse-market.

Here was the Jewish center of trade, the heart of the town. Among the low wooden houses with shingled roofs, close one to another as if one mother had given birth to them, stood Zelig Yudes' two-story red brick house (actually the only one in town).

On both sides there stretched a row of poplar trees between which was a broad, paved path of pointy stones. The mountain grew out of the middle of the town and was famous in the area. Around it curved the little Panizer Street where the houses were built into the mountainside. From this street smaller streets stretched in the direction of the river and each carried the name of an important resident, such as Yude Velvl's Street, Eli Nosn's, Moshe the Painter's and others. In the center was the synagogue courtyard where were concentrated all the members of the clergy and poverty of the town, as well as all the community buildings such as the ritual bath, the poorhouse, the Talmud Torah which later served as the elementary school and for many years as the location for all Zionist organizations. From Moshe the Painter's Street, the Russian Street stretched past the river on the way to the cemetery. From the horse-market on the other end of town began the large Rubelyaner Street with its orchards which served as a place for the town residents to stroll.

[Page 28]

The River

by Herzl Weiner

Translated by Mindle Crystel Gross

Edited by Toby Bird z"l

Our town was blessed with its own unique riches of nature. The mountain looked huge and majestic with its head cut off. It was reflected in the quiet water of the river. The river's history began hundreds of years earlier after many large changes of nature on the earth. Many rivers were created in the Vilna area, as well as the Svir River. In town it was called the lake, but it was actually a river of which we had nothing to be ashamed. It was considered to be the third largest in the Vilna area. From the south, it joined via a narrow canal to the Vishnever River, and from the east it incorporated the waters from flowing canals. It was 14 km long and its broadest point was opposite the town where it was 5 km. It then became narrower behind town and ended up in a small shallow river which was named the Reke, where the water seldom froze and was crystal-clear. This served as the place to bathe for a portion of the town. The Reke emptied into the Vile and together flowed into the Nyeman and then eventually reached the Baltic Sea.

On the opposite side, peasant villages were immersed in green meadows where cows grazed. Young forests stretched along the shore.

1 ½ km from town, surrounded on three sides, by water, was the cemetery.

[Page 29]

The Bridge

by Herzl Weiner

Translated by Mindle Crystel Gross

Edited by Toby Bird z"l

The bridge was the beginning and the end of the town. On the other side – green meadows were spread out in all their glory, continuing far on the golden waves of thick, deep forests which rimmed the horizon in a dark frame. Across from this spread out a huge swamp where nobody could come on foot. Frogs croaked there all winter long. During autumn, poor peasants cried bitter tears about this stretch because it could not be avoided and because of this, the town was cut off from the world and no railroad line could reach there.

From here, a narrow sandy path led out to the broader world.

New beliefs fired up young minds. The shine of a dream of a future tomorrow mesmerized them – caught them in the net of the rising red dawn.

From here the first tentative step was taken, and with eyes open wide at the world's huge arms, they fell in, blinded by the surrounding spreading light.

Tens of Jewish boys and girls were thus led away.

Here on the bridge, each who left the town was escorted with hands clasped warmly and hot tears pouring. Here marriages were celebrated and jealousy accompanied those who left.

From here, one had the last view of those sad and remaining-behind fathers and mothers, and also the dearly loved little town.

Here, for the last time, I bade goodbye to my dear ones. To this very day I can still see on that summer day, my mother's sad face and tear-filled eyes. They follow me like shadows. Her last words to me slice through my heart like knives. My brother's shout – don't forget us… Oh, my dear ones, I never imagined that the knife was already lying upon your necks. I will never meet you again and the other dear Jews who came to escort me.

The bridge was also the most loved romantic corner for the town's young people. After walking across the long bridge, one would get hit in the face with a delicious freshness, a strong aroma of the green growth all about. There were many more pleasures all around, like leaning on the balustrade of the bridge and listening to the quiet murmur of the slapping waves beneath it. Sometimes, the stillness would be interrupted by the music of guitars and mandolins joined in joyful song and the echoing laughter of young folk who had wandered here late at night on a little boat.

The bridge was burned during WWI and immediately rebuilt. It emerged intact from the war. All of the Jews were marched across it on their final way.

In the little town
My mother bore me.
On the mountain
My childhood years played out
And I left them today forever
Black sorrow enveloped them.

[Page 31]

Svirer Life According to the *Vilner Pinkes*, YEKOPO

Translated by Mindle Crystel Gross

Edited by Toby Bird z"l

The Vilna Yekopo [an acronym for Jewish Relief Committee for War Victims] in 1931, published a separate *pinkas* [register] under the title "Upon the Destruction of War and Turmoil." On pg. 387 was printed the following correspondence about Svir:

"The main occupation of the Jews of Svir is shopkeeping and small business. Their situation is not good. There is an overflow of shops. The income is low. Market day is once a week – every Thursday. At that time, many shopkeepers arrive from the entire province and due to their cheap competition prices, they undermine the livelihood of the Jewish shopkeepers.

Because of this, our grain trade went under. The peasant does not have what to sell, so their Jewish village tradesmen must suffer greatly, who are here in Svir in substantial numbers.

Also the Jewish craftsmen are out of work and poor.

75% of the Jewish population receives aid from relatives and friends in America. This virtually helps the town to sustain its life in any way possible.

R' Moshe Miller's little boat
(Jewish fisherman)

[Page 35]

Chapter Two

The Cultural and Social Life

A Cultural and Social *Shtetele*

by Chanoch Drutz

Translated by Mindle Crystel Gross

Edited by Toby Bird z"l

Svir was considered to be an intelligent town within the entire Vilna province.

The Jewish population was divided into two camps: Zionists and anti-Zionists. The Zionists, for the most part, congregated around the He'khalutz and Tseirey Tsiyon, and only a few were "general" Zionists and revisionists. The anti--Zionists belonged to the Bund or to the White Russian Communist party.

After WWI, there was a stubborn battle about the elementary school. The Zionists, however, emerged the victors and there existed in Svir a Tarbut school the entire time.

The Synagogue

**Rav H'Gaon R'Naftali Dovid Mosevzon,
of blessed memory**

Nevertheless, we could not ignore the Yiddishist camp, because a portion of the intelligentsia centered itself around them. There were almost no assimilated in Svir, and very rarely and only in very few homes, did Jews speak Russian or Polish. That is why Svir was proud of its pure folk Yiddish, and even the most extreme adherents of the Tarbut school loved Yiddish and Jewish culture.

In Svir, the open "trials" were much loved as were the so-called "box" evenings. Various types of questions would be thrown into the box and the leaders of the different sides answered them. The questions were mostly of a literary and historical nature, but quite often, a piquant question would be asked and the audience would later joke about it.

Svir halutzim in 1932

In general, it was a rarity that a Friday evening or a Shabes should be without a gathering. Speakers loved to visit Svir because they always found an attentive audience. It almost never happened in Svir that a speaker would arrive and find an empty hall. There would always be an audience.

Svir earned its good name because of its cultural and social institutions which were always on a high level.

Svir was known for its excellent library, which in recent years had 1,000 books. We must comment that until 1918, there was no library in Svir. It was only after WWI that many tens of books were brought to Svir by Eliyohu Rabinovitz. With this, the foundation was laid for the later Svir people's library.

The funds were raised through various performances and other contributions. The entire youth, Yiddishists and Zionists, became united in order to enlarge the library. The initiative, however, always came from Henekh Miller.

There was almost no family in Svir who did not subscribe to a newspaper. If somebody did not have enough money, he partnered with somebody else. There were cases of three families subscribing together to one newspaper, but all read a daily newspaper. That is why Svir was considered to be a knowledgeable town.

The Vilna newspapers were read in Svir: *Tsayt* and *Tog*; the Warsaw newspapers: *Haynt* and *Folks' Newspaper* and the weekly *Literary Pages* and *Folk Health*.

The first to bring newspapers to Svir were Zolye Zlatayavke and Avrum Yitskhok Miller. Later on, Henekh Miller became involved and distributed newspapers around town.

Members of HaShomer HaTzair 1925

Sviri Hehalutz 1925

In general, it is worthwhile to note that the well-developed newspaper business owes its success in Svir to the Miller brothers, Avram Yitzhak, Heinich and Oyzer.

Soon the Hehalutz organized a reading room and opened, where we could find not only a daily newspaper but journals and monthly publications.

Of great interest were the journals which the youth of Svir themselves published. Thanks to the reading room, these written journals were read by tens of friends.

Quite often, lectures would take place in Svir. There were a number of good Zionist speakers who lived in Svir. Among those who distinguished themselves with their interesting lectures were the teachers Rogov and Yakov Dov Gordon, the rabbi's son-in-law, and Shloyme Kreitser, and from the Yiddishists – Eliyohu Zlatayavke.

There were also frequent literary evenings. The best were about Mendele's *Taksi,* about *God of Revenge*, and *Motek the Thief*, the famous work by Sholem Ash.

In the entire province of Sventsiyon, Svir was noted for its dramatic circles. The Svir theatre performances were on a high artistic plain and were not just a play for those who loved theatre.

The first theatre performance took place in 1916 with the presentation of Gordon's play, *Hertzele Meyuchas* [lit. of distinguished lineage], at the home of Yose Moshe Ber.

Bentsye Yudl acted in this performance as *Mikhl the Matchmaker*. The other chief roles were played by: Yisroel Alperovitch, Shloyme Ayzerovitz, Eliyohu Rabinovitz, Kisenye Gordon, Berte Berson, Pere Kaplan and Bat-Sheva Svirsky, Yone the ironwork's owner's daughter. The director was one Berman, a refugee from Vileyke.

The fee went to feed the poor.

The performance was a great success and even the officers were enthusiastic about it.

After the war, thanks to the initiative of Bukhhalter, Shimon Rozaler, a second group was founded with other performers. Yisroel Lev Shvartzgar, Hershl Miller, Shmuel Resnick, Avrum Kaplan, Yosef Chaim and the women, Rivka Ayzikov, Khaye Vayler, Batya Fisher, Bat-Sheva Yaffe, Sheyne Reyzl Yaffe and Khana Kissin all belonged to this group.

The director, Shimon Rozaler, also acted in Vilna in a drama group. He opened an office in Svir for requests and the residents of Svir have much for which to thank him.

The most important plays which were performed on the Svir stage were:

    Gordon's *The Wild Man*
    Dvoyrele Meyuchas
    The Slaughter
    Khassye the Orphan
    Kobrin's *The Village Youth*
    Tsipke Fayer
    Lovke Maladyetz

Peretz Hirshbeyn's *The Carcass, The Intelligent One*
Viktor Hugo's *The Rich Man in Chains*
Sholem Ash's *Motke the Thief*
Tankeler's *The Bridegroom* (Joseph Tunkel)
Tankeler's *Bells* (Joseph Tunkel)
Where Are My Children?
The Big Moment
Moliere's *The Miser*
The Empty Inn
Mote Melekh the Carpenter
Sholem Aleikhem's *Two Hundred Thousand*
The Divorce
Yizkor
The Seven Who Were Hanged

Motke the Thief produced by the drama group 1931

Outstanding in serious roles were: Yisroel Zev Shvartsgar, Berl Goldman, Avrum Kaplan, Rokhl Vayler, Basye Fisher, Bat-Sheva Yaffe and Sheyne Reyzl Yaffe. Excelling in comedy were: Heshl Miller, Shmuel Resnick and Yosef Khayt.

The greatest difficulty for the Svir actors was that they did not have a suitable venue. It was crowded at Yose Moyshe Ber's, and in Fayve Svirsky's stable it was cold, and at Velvl Drutz's, it was larger but also not comfortable. So the decision was made to build a stage in the women's shul and perform there. You understand, that all preparations had to be made in secret because they knew that the orthodox would not have permitted it.

Finally, in 1927, they built the big hall in the fire-fighters' building and there they built a permanent stage.

From that time on, Svir had a proper theatre.

As long as all the youth was united in one drama group, things ran smoothly. When the money that was paid went to the folk-library and the fire-fighters, everybody was in agreement, but when He'khalutz began to demand a portion of the money for khalutzim who did not have the money for aliya to Eretz Yisroel, the Yiddisists agreed to form a separate drama group.

That is how two drama groups developed in Svir.

Nevertheless, Svir sought methods for uniting the two, and soon found them. This was *The Tournament and Sports Club*, *The Guardians of the Sick* and the orchestra.

The initiative to establish a Tournament organization in Svir came from Berl Alperovitz. He was an avid sportsman and had many theoretical and practical ideas about sports.

The Tournament and Sports Club was named *Maccabee* and was connected to the central *Maccabee* organization of Poland. The instructor was Berl Alperovitz.

They rented a place for practice at Chaim Moyshe Rabinovitz' and a football field was fixed up behind the Polish cemetery.

The Svir football players quickly earned a good name in the province. They defeated not only Mikhaleyshak, but even Smarna, and with Sventsyon, they remained tied. Yulke Motskin excelled as goalkeeper; defending were Avrum Kaplan and Berl Resnick; intercepting were Heshl Miller, Chanan Epshtayn and Yitskhok Resnick; opponents were Yosef Kamin, Avrum Yitskhok Miller, Leybl Moller, Lolye Zlatayavke and Pinkhas Hazan.

In addition to the football players, Svir also had divisions for light and difficult athletics.

Svir Hehalutz in 1931

The Tournament and Sports Club lost its role in the life of Svir at the beginning of the 1930's. Berl Alperovitz went to Paris, Yosef Kamin went to Argentina and many other players left to Eretz Israel. Among them was also the best player of the second group, Khanon Weiner.

The arrests of the Communists robbed the Sport Club of one of its main strengths, Yulke Motzkin, the Svir goal-keeper.

All this caused the downfall of the great football club.

Svir *the Guardians of the Sick*

A beautiful, beloved and worthwhile institution which also helped to unite all levels was *The Guardians of the Sick*.

The initiative for this institution was Elyakim Kovorski. While sitting in his house on one occasion, discussing various tragedies which had befallen residents of Svir, the thought occurred that the entire burden should not be carried by the family members. The youth of Svir must help. The help is most necessary at night because the family caregivers must also rest and there is no hospital in Svir, nor nurses. Therefore, every night another couple of people must be sent to help and watch the patient.

It did not take much thought in Svir – said and done.

A general meeting was immediately called of the entire Svir youth, not differentiating between party or direction.

Velvl Drutz, one of the active members of The Guardians of the Sick, his wife, Sore, daughter and son-in-law

Elikim Kovarski spoke about the proposal, and after a short discussion, it was accepted with enthusiasm.

At the first meeting were elected: Elikim Kovarski, Moyshe Drevyatski, Berl Alperovitz, Shmuel Resnick, Heshl Miller, Ruven Meyer Resnick and Abba Weiner.

A short time later, it was decided that they could not do with only sending people at night to the sick. Very often, a doctor must be brought and free medicine to the indigent sick supplied. They thought about how to raise the necessary funds.

Mostly, the money was raised through theatre performances, but the administration also created other sources.

This is how The Guardians of the Sick took upon themselves the task of baking matzos for Passover. All the friends obligated themselves to work without pay. Some worked as the one who put the matzo into the oven, others as the one who made the perforations, others to roll out the dough. Most importantly, so many people gave The Guardians the chore of baking their matzo that the revenue from this was quite significant. It is worthwhile mentioning that Elye Rabinovitz permitted his house to be used for such an important purpose.

In the list of those who were sick for whom the members of the Guardians provided night after night, for months serving with devotion, we note Rabbi Mosevzon, Velvl Drutz, Minnie Fisher and many others.

The Svir Orchestra

After the big fire at Fayvl Svirsky's house, the firefighters group strengthened in Svir. Each homeowner gave ten zlotys and quite a large sum was collected.

After long deliberations, the administration decided to establish a wind orchestra. Since they had approximately 1200 zlotys, they bought 14 instruments. This was not enough because 15 people had signed up for the orchestra, so they were divided into two groups and they began to study.

The Svir Wind Orchestra 1930

The first director was Elikim Kovarski. Later on, they hired a Christian from Smarna and still later, Zalman Alpert took over the reins and finally, at the end, Perl Resnick.

The Svir orchestra participated in all the celebrations of the town, as well as Jewish-national celebrations. Above all, it met with great success at the welcome celebration for president Mestitskin.

In 1935, the Svir orchestra attended the first May demonstrations in Vilna. Since all the members were Socialists, nobody refused to go. In the Subatch kibbutz, they met up with those from Sventsiyon.

On the corner of Vilna and Metzkevitz Streets, they were attacked by a group of hooligans and were badly beaten.

From that time on, the orchestra performed only in Svir. During the winter, the rehearsals were held in the elementary school and in Saray during the summer.

In the last years before WWII, the orchestra was composed of the best talents of the Svir youth.

Among the most talented orchestra members were: Aaron Gitlin, Akiva Fisher, Nakhum Shrayer, Yekhiel Miller, Zelig Rabinovitz, the brothers Moyshe and Noyakh Alperovitz and others.

You understand, of course, that everybody played without being paid.

They were rewarded for this by living to enjoy pleasure because their efforts were not for naught. The orchestra quickly developed into one of the best institutions in Svir and became a part of Svir's cultural and social life.

[Page 48 - Yiddish]

The People's Library

By Herzl Weiner

Translated by Mindle Crystel Gross

Edited by Toby Bird z"l

The library in Svir was established right about the end of WWI, and it is thanks to the initiative of Eli Rabinovitch and actual help from Yekopo which set as its goal not only to rescue us from the economic ruin, but at the same time, to elevate the cultural level in town. With a total of 12 books, the foundation was laid for the people's library in Khatskelevitch's house, and later grew to be one of the largest libraries in the area with close to 3,000 books and a broad selection of various Yiddish and Hebrew volumes. They encompassed the classics and modern Jewish literature and also those translated from other languages, including many scientific works and assorted timely journals. The Jewish youth, enjoying the various novels, immersed itself in the rich well of the newly-grown Yiddish literature and enriched their knowledge. The Jewish town was poor and the people carried much spiritual baggage at that time, and the library was a window which opened wide onto the horizon of the surrounding bright world, and which broke through the narrowness of the small town, preparing the foundation for the latest events of the political parties and organizations in town. During the early years, the library was run by the so-called Yiddishist camp, like A. Zlatayavke, M. Drevyatski and others. Later, however, with the strengthening of the Zionist organizations, they participated in the administration and they worked with the brothers Alperovitz, Chanoch Miller, Sore Tsakh, Eliyohu Epshteyn, Moyshe Miller, Yehuda Gershovitz, and the writer of these lines, as well as others. It was a joint effort and pleasant years were enjoyed by both sides for the continuation and development of the library. Many theatre performances which raised funds were dedicated to the library and presented an opportunity to purchase books.

Herzl Weiner and his mother

There was also an intensive cultural effort conducted, such as establishing "box" evenings, where the so-called elite of the town would answer questions. They were B. Alperovitz, A. Zlatayavke, Kh. Rogov, Y. Engle, and others, including teachers who came later. Many serious questions were posed, scientific, political and literary, which troubled the minds of the youth, and which found their immediate answers. Also arranged were many literary evening "trials" which had a valuable influence on the upbringing of the young, like Mendele's *Taksi*, Peretz's *Bontche Shvayg*, and Sholem Ash's *God of Revenge*, and others.

Especially notable was the trial of the *Woman* which drew in a large number of participants and lasted for two months. The accusers, Y. Gordon and Y. Engle, were supported by Ita Vayniger and Strindberg. The defendants were supported by Y. Motzkin and B. Z. Malamyak to defend the non-Soviet literature. At the end, after hearing the witnesses for both sides, the verdict was announced by the tribunal and the woman speaks freely and accuses the community which had enslaved her and cast her out from life's better positions.

The "trial" resulted in great interest and left a deep impression in town.

The last years with the greatest number of active youth leaving the town, some to Eretz Yisroel, others immigrating to other countries, a simultaneous weakening in the work of all the parties in town. Once again, the library fulfilled its function as the spiritual center and concentrated around itself the creative talents. Thanks to the energetic administration and the initiative of B. Resnick and A. Zlatayovke, they were successful in obtaining through various methods, a radio, something very precious at that time, and the only one in town for the Jewish community. It ran on batteries as there was not yet any electricity in town. This created the possibility of listening for hours to various programs from the entire world, such as music, song and daily news from Poland. Most importantly, they found a strong interest in the Jewish programs from the Soviet Union, and with trembling joy, listened to every second and word from faraway Eretz Yisroel, which is so dear and to which everybody is tied organically and wants to go there. The youth enjoyed the broadcast music, dancing late into the night, a lovely cultural happening in town.

With the outbreak of the war, the library, along with the entire spiritual life of the community, was destroyed.

[Page 51 - Yiddish]

The First Elementary School in Svir

by Shmuel Dobkin

Translated by Mindle Crystel Gross

Edited by Toby Bird z"l

The founding of the first elementary school in our town was a great happening and created a revolution in our education and upbringing.

This took place a couple of years after WWI. People began to breathe easier, new birds began to sing new songs, ideals about freedom, equality and national freedom were felt in the air, and people began to believe in a better tomorrow.

At that time, the first school was founded in town, and we saw in it the beginning of a new era, a better one, a more beautiful one. The first two teachers themselves were former students, consumed with the idea of going to the people to teach them, educate them, threw themselves with great fervor into organizing the school and situating it on a new pedagogic and modern foundation. They began to create something out of nothing. They did not have at their disposition the good will of the parents, and the enthusiasm of the children to learn. They tested all the future students and created the classes. The yeshiva building near the synagogue was turned into a place for the school, and we, the children, began with great joy and enthusiasm to learn there. Everything was a great revelation for us. We studied only five-six hours a day, with a break after each lesson during which time we played in the courtyard, jumping and running. In addition to the Jewish studies, we also studied general subjects, e.g.: arithmetic, geography, science, music and so forth. The lessons themselves were not taught the way they were in kheder The teacher had conversations with the children in our language and asked questions. The teacher later reviewed everything and it all became clear. The new school books that we received elicited great happiness and respect from us. We began to feel that the school was unfolding a new world for us, a real one, a substantial one, and it was eager to connect us with it, and to interest us in this large world.

The school taught us to recognize nature around us, the trees, the fields and meadows, and maybe to love them as well and to give thought to the entire development-process of the larger surroundings.

The respect for these first two teachers was great. Their word is holy to us. The school becomes the cultural center of the town.

In the history of the Jewish education in our town, the first elementary school will be noted as having been an important contributor to our social and cultural success.

The first Hebrew School in Svir

Chaim Rugovin

Translated by Sara Mages

[Page 53]

I'd reached old age, because our Sages said in Avot [5:21] "at sixty to be an elder", and when I do the account of my life, I add the establishment of the Hebrew School in Svir, one of the most important enterprises of my life, to my account. Now, when the memory of Svir's Jewry with all of its institutions has been uprooted from the world, the review of the past will give us the opportunity to appreciate the historical value of the Hebrew School. This school taught boys and girls to love the Jewish people and the land of Israel. This school prepared the hearts before the storm, which destroyed almost all of the European Jewry, and in my opinion, it was the biggest factor that a very large percentage survived the decrees and the Holocaust from such a small town. If the TSYSHO School (Tsentrale Yidishe Shul-Organizatsye - central Yiddish school organization), that I found at the beginning of 1921, remained, it would have turned the hearts of its graduates to travel and escape to Stalin and his friends' Evil Kingdom. To what can this be compared? to people who survived the fire and fell into deep water, "none who go to her return again" [the Book of Proverbs 2:19].

I came to Vilna in the winter of 1921 with a small suitcase in my hand and about 200 Polish Marks in my pocket. Of course, I lacked a Polish document that I was resident of the district of Vilna. By chance, I met a man on the street who knew me and my family from Minsk. I told him about my hardships, and what happened to me since I escaped from the "Bolsheviks" in Minsk. He went with me to the Jewish community. I saw that many clerks and the head of the community, the old Dr. Vigodski, knew him. There, he met another man and said to him: "we both go and testify about this man", and pointed his finger at me. I introduced myself to the stranger and both of them approached one of the clerks. The clerk swore them on their testimony that I'm a decent honest man. The clerk wrote a document in Polish, stamped it with the community's seal, and Dr. Vigodski signed it. I felt more secure walking in the streets with this kosher amulet. The days were the days of the government of the Polish General Zygowski. The Jews, who lived in the district of Vilna, were afraid of the slightest noise. The general tried to show himself as a liberal, and was cordial to Jewish community of Vilna in order

[Page 54]

to distract their minds from his political trickery, to rip the district of Vilna from Lita - where the Jews enjoyed all the civil rights – and annex it to the Polish government.

I went to the Hebrew teachers' center to ask for a job. There, they told me that there were too many Hebrew teachers in Vilna, the roads around Vilna were too dangerous, and the teachers' center had no clear information about Hebrew schools in small towns. When I told them that the Polish Marks are shrinking in my pocket, they advised me to go to TSYSHO, because sometimes they need a "cure", a Hebrew teacher.

Without a choice, and against my will, I went to TSYSHO. There, they told me that they received a request for a Hebrew teacher from their school in Svir, who will teach Hebrew in Yiddish but not Hebrew in Hebrew. They informed me that the school already has a teacher for general studies and the Polish language, and they recognize her as the principal. They also let it slip, that the Polish superintendent in the province city of Švenèionys refuses to confirm her. They asked me about my knowledge in general studies. I showed them my papers from the Russian secondary school in Minsk, and since the Poles controlled Minsk for about a year, there was a also a Polish stamp on them.

Before I left Vilna, I revisited the center of *"Tzeirei Zion"* [Young Zionists] movement. They asked me to write them on the status of the youth in the town of Svir, maybe they'll be able to establish a branch of *"Tzeirei Zion"* there. They also told me that a "Tarbut" [a network of secular Hebrew-language schools] center will be established soon. Menachem Rudnicki arrived, or fled from Moscow, and he'll head the center. Then, they'll establish Hebrew schools in small towns, and wage a war against TSYSHO in the provinces.

In the Svirim's hostel, in Rivka Solowizik's home, they told that on the same night, a dark rainy night, a convoy of carts will leave for Svir. I told one of the carters that I don't have the money to pay for the trip, but I was sure that the school's management will pay him. He agreed to take me. I remember that Polie Seirski and his brother Yitzchak were also members of the caravan. At night we were stopped by the police. They searched the carts, my suitcase, my pockets, and also frisked me. The document from the community wasn't good enough for them, and by miracle they didn't stop me. On the second night, a snowy night, one of the nights of the month of Shevat 1921, we finally arrived to Henie Kaplan's home.

[Page 55]

They told me to get off there. It was about an hour before midnight. Shulamit, the school principal, also lived in Henie's home. She slept in the same room with Perale, Henie's stepdaughter, and I slept in the dining room. The first homeowner to greet me was Zalman Michel Fisher. On the next day I started to teach at the school. The intellectual climate of the school was foreign to my liking, and the Hebrew studies were at a low level. When we returned from school, I sat down to eat together with Shulamit. She asked my opinion about the school. I expressed my opinion that we should correct the studies of our nation's history, and give the children a positive attitude towards our actions and hopes in our homeland. During the conversation I realized that we were students of foreign worlds, and opposed each other.

Meanwhile, I met good innocent people who cared about me, like Zev Drutz. None of them suspected that I didn't like their school.

Teachers Chaim Rugovin and Chaim Gershater

[Page 56]

I was alone and lonely. I wanted to rent a special room for myself so I won't have to sleep in the dining room, and they told me that there was no such thing in town.

After the holiday of Purim, the principal Shulamit traveled to Švenèionys to see the Polish inspector in charge of the district's schools, and took my papers to confirm me as a teacher. When she returned she surprised me. The inspector confirmed me as a principal and her as a teacher, because he didn't find anything wrong with my papers. He sent me an official certificate that I was the official school's principal. From that time, the district supervisor turned to me in all the official negotiations about the school, even though I didn't know Polish. This fact angered TSYSHO.

Those were the days of commercial prosperity because of the depreciation of the Polish Mark. The whole town was busy trading and exchanging money from Dollars to Marks and vice versa. A young man came and said that he was a dance teacher, and all the youth joined him and began to dance at night.

The month of Nisan arrived and brought the spring winds. I started to miss the friendship of people my age because the homeowners, who come to visit me, were older than me by many years. One day, at the beginning of Nisan, as I sat alone in the dining room, Perale's brother came and told me that a youth delegation want to talk to me. I received them amicably. We talked, and from the conversation I learned that the town's youth grew during the war, during the days of chaos. Apart from the knowledge that they have acquired in the old "*Heder*", they had almost no education. They heard about the Zionist movements, but their concepts weren't clear to them. They wander through life and eager for a different intellectual world. In short, they wanted me to guide them, organize them and be their mentor. I took this job with great joy. At first, I organized a branch of "*Tzeirei Zion*". I wanted to establish a platform and support if I decide to wage a war against the Yiddish School. At the beginning the branch wasn't big. Among the members were: Reuven Reznik, Isaac Tzakh, and May they live - Yisrael Wele Schwartz who lives in the United States, and Chaim Chaiat who was the first pioneer to immigrate from Svir to Israel. The last was

[Page 57]

Chana Rugovin's parents, Mina and Zalman Eliyahu Swirski of blessed memory

knowledgeable in Hebrew and Yiddish literature more than anyone else. I wanted to expand the branch and attract the fathers and mothers, the parents of the school children.

To carry out my wish, we decided that I should speak from the synagogue's Holy Ark *Bimah* wrapped in a prayer shawl. We chose the Sabbath of *Parashat "Aharei Mot"* ["After the death" Torah portion]. On Friday eve we hung a notice in the synagogue that I'll speak an hour before *Mincha* prayer. On that Sabbath, the *Shamash* called the congregation to come to the synagogue after their afternoon nap. As in Rosh Hashanah, the synagogue and the women's section were full of people. My subject was "strange fire" – which is mentioned in the same *Parasha*. The impression was great, and on the next day we sold one hundred "*Tzeirei Zion*" shekels [memberships]. Many asked us to sign them as members of "*Tzeirei Zion*". I think about fifty men and women signed up. Many important homeowners started to visit me regularly like: Zev Drutz, Nachman Gurvitz, Spekter and the like. We started to meet almost every Saturday, and the number of participants increased.

[Page 58]

I chose a subject: Hebrew or Yiddish? Shulamit was frightened. She suddenly realized that TSYSHO made a mistake hiring me. The Yidishe [Yiddish speaking] started to organize. Their friends were of various types: *Bundistim*, communists, and just "those who don't know to ask". In my opinion, their biggest shortcoming was that they didn't have a leader and a manager. Shulamit couldn't give a speech, and so were the other teachers from TSYSHO.

The first quarrel that broke out between us was in early May of the same year (1921). The Polish authority turned to me, the official school principal, with a request that we won't teach on May third, their Constitution Day. They asked that Shulamit and I will organize the children in rows, and march in a procession through the main street to a location near the Christian Church where the Polish School children will also gather. I agreed to participate in this procession, but suggested that our school will march with our national blue and white flag. The Polish delegates promised me that they would bring this condition before the celebration committee. On May second I received a positive answer. When Shulamit heard it, her face reddened from anger. She screamed very loudly: "The Jews don't have a flag. Our flag is the flag of this country, the Polish flag, the blue and white flag is the flag of the Zionist's dream". Time was short because it was already the evening of May second, and on the next day, at nine o'clock in morning, we had to march. I called Yisrael Wele Schwartz and Chaim Chaiat, and they decided that all the members of "*Tzeirei Zion*", mostly the female members, will come to school immediately. Shortly after, I had a big blue and white flag in my hands, and dozens of small blue and white flags for the children to hold in their hands. Our school's May third procession was festive. After their schools sang the Polish national anthem, our children sang "*Hatikvah*", and we sang it again when we returned to the anger of the Yidishe. I think that many former students, who now live in Israel, remember this festive occasion and the impression that it left on the town.

Since then, I started to demand publicly that the Yiddish School should be demolished and a Hebrew "Tarbut" School will be established. Almost all the homeowners, whose children studied in the school, supported me. Then, I slowly began to lay the foundation for Hebrew in Hebrew.

[Page 59]

I decided to prepare the most talented students, Chanoch Drutz, the two Yoel brothers, Sutzkewer, Dubkin and others, and increase their vocabulary. They probably didn't understand why I gave them more work. Very important public work was done until the summer vacation. Large meetings were held every Saturday and I spoke about various international issues, especially about the treasures of the Hebrew language. That spring "*Tzeirei Zion*" held a conference in Vilna, and I was sent as a delegate. The economic situation in town wasn't bad, and most of the parents paid tuition. Once, YEKOPO [an aid organization for Jewish victims of war] received a few hundred dollars from America, which were exchanged to tens of thousands of Polish Marks. They also donated money to the school in Svir. Central Lita wasn't annexed to Poland yet, and for the sake of appearance they continued to maintain the international contract, and sometimes donated money to the national minority schools. Therefore, the school in Svir also received a few thousands Marks. I also received my salary, which was four thousands Marks a month. They also paid me for all the vacation days – I don't remember – six weeks or two months. In the month of Elul 1921, I left Svir because I got a job in the municipal "Talmud Torah" school in Vilna, which was one of *Mizrachi's* schools. .

My hopes that made me move to Vilna dashed very slowly. The parents of the children, who came from Svir to Vilna for their business, persuaded me to return to Svir, remove the school from the ownership of TSYSHO, transfer it to the ownership of "Tarbut", and be its principal. In Svir, the teachers were paid ten thousands Marks a month, more than in Vilna. Even my wife Chana begged me to return to Svir. All these things influenced me. In Vilna I was only a teacher, and in Svir I was going to create something new. I consulted with the director of the institute, because I trusted him, and he answered me: "Do as you wish, but my heart is telling me that you'll regret it". I thought it over and made a crucial decision, to return to Svir and establish a "Tarbut" School there. I think I returned in the month of Adar 1922. All the residents of the town received me with love and affection, and of course, the Yidishe camp wasn't happy with me. I had a lot of work to do: I started to correct and modify the curriculum, and corresponded with the "Tarbut" office in Vilna in the matter of a second teacher.

[Page 60]

I also reorganize the branch of *"Tzeirei Zion"*, which has weakened during my absence from Svir, because I knew that the federation would support me and the school. A second teacher arrived after Passover. He was a good teacher, who influenced the children by organizing sports games, a subject that I wasn't familiar with.

The Yidishe camp wanted to get rid of me. They believed that if I left the town, they would seize the school building and everything will return to normal. There were a number of thugs among them who informed the kingdom that came from Russia, and every Jew who came from Russia was a Russian spy in the eyes of the Polish government. In the month of Elul of the same year (1922), I celebrated my wedding feast, and before the seven days of the feast ended I was summoned to the police for an investigation. The Yidishe camp was jubilant and happy. The Polish passport, which I've acquired, was taken from me. I started to wander from Svir to Švenèionys, and from here to there. I was interrogated by police, and I was in danger of expulsion from Poland to Russia. Returning to Russia was equal to a capital punishment, because I escaped from there and my name was blacklisted. It is difficult to describe the troubles that the informers caused me. It took me almost a year to obtain a valid Polish passport.

Despite all the troubles, the Hebrew School continued to evolve, and most of the students succeeded in their studies.

Meanwhile, the economic situation of the Jews in Poland has worsened, including the Jews of Svir. Of course, it also affected the financial situation of the school. The value of the Polish Mark fell, and the teachers demanded a pay raise. When the days of Grabeski, may his name be blotted out, started, the Polish Jews lost their livelihood. It was difficult to pay tuition, and I, the "swindler", the principal of the school in Svir, was forced to demand salaries for me and for the other teachers. The leaders of *"Tzeirei Zion"* like Yisrael Wele Schwartz, Chaim Chaiat, Issac Schwartz and others decided to intervene. They realized that the Hebrew School, which they helped to built, is going to be destroyed. They took it on themselves to collect the teachers' salaries - and Yisrael Wele Schwartz was elected as treasurer. If my memory serves me, there was a fundraiser for the school in the form of a school play.

[Page 61]

Members of Tarbut school in Svir – 1925
[Tarbut – Zionist network of Hebrew educational institutions founded in 1922]

The financial resources of *"Tzeirei Zion"* were temporary, and I saw that it was difficult for them to carry the burden. Since I realized that if I left the school it would remain Hebrew and a "Tarbut" institution, I decided during the vacation days of 1925 to leave the school in Svir, and look for a job in another town, and so I have done.

In the month of Elul of the same year (1925), I was accepted as a teacher in Dokshiz, a town four times larger than Svir. The school was also founded by "Tarbut" - but it was more established because there was an organized community there. There were also a number of affluent educated people in the community. There were four teachers. The Polish language teacher was also the principal, who was sent from "Tarbut", but what happened to me in Svir also happened to me here. The Polish superintended appointed me as the official school principal. Also there, I revived the chapters of *"Tzeirei Zion"* and *"HeHalutz"*. At the end of the year they kept me for the next year. Meanwhile, I received an opportunity to travel to the United States. I traveled from Dokshiz to Vilna, where I taught at the Hebrew High School for two months, and at the end of November (1926) I left Poland and traveled to America.

I don't know what happened at the school in Svir since the vacation days of 1925, but one thing is clear, the school remained a Hebrew School and continued what I started,

[Page 62]

to build, in the spirit of Hebrew language, a productive home for future generations who would be closely connected to our ancient new country.

San Francisco, California, United States – 18 Adar 5718

[Page 62 - Yiddish]

The Svir Gymnastics and Sports Club

by Berl Alperovitz

Translated by Mindle Crystel Gross

Edited by Toby Bird z"l

…A Gymnastics Club in Svir? What kind of nonsense is this? Something like this had never been heard of before! This is some kind of punishment from heaven… Strong young men who should already be thinking about their future, about marriage, about a store come and allow themselves to be led by a young know-it-all from Germany. He teaches them how to march, about face, tumble and various other tricks – exactly like crazy people. And this – beneath the free sky, in the middle of the day, at the horse-market, and they aren't even embarrassed…

Such were the atmosphere, the impressions and opinions about the new institution for physical education of the Jewish youth in Svir. The Gymnastics Club was then the sensation of the day. It was discussed in every home, and about which the "polite" people spoke in disparaging terms.

A gathering and a discussion.

I called for an organizing gathering at which I spoke about the goal and importance of physical education for the Jewish youth. Almost all of those present – about 30 – signed up as members. A committee was chosen, comprised of: Shloyme Hirsh Ayzikovitch, Paule Svirsky, Eli Rabinovitch, and others. They became the founders and activists of the Club. Later, there also was founded a girls' group. The most active participants in the girls' group were Khane Kissin and Yokhe Fisher.

Svir football players of Maccabee in 1923

Not yet having any permission from the authorities, the first couple of classes were conducted under the aegis of the fire-fighters at their locale. This brought out the anger of the homeowners to such a degree, that they called a gathering, maintaining thatI was leading the youth of Svir away from the right path. One fine day, I was approached by the shames who, trembling from fear, tells me: "I have come to report you in the name of the homeowners, that you should cease your tricks. If you do not, they have decided at a gathering to turn to the authorities with a petition that you be sent out of Svir". With these final words, the old shames began to tremble even more.

The football players of Svir – 1931

Seeing that things were progressing well, and the members came regularly for their lessons, we decided to get in contact with the Maccabee in Vilna and requested their help with instruction material and so forth. To this purpose, the directors delegated Eli Rabinovitch to go to Vilna. Upon his return, he enthusiastically reported to the administration about the reception they had given him at the Vilna Macabee, how amazed the local instructors were when they heard about a Gymnastics Club in Svir at a time when the Vilna Maccabee was itself still young.

First of all, the Vilna Maccabee gave him gymnastic lesson-books and promised to send any necessary gymnastic equipment, which actually did arrive quite quickly – a bench and a ladder.

On February 21st, 1922, they gave us formal permission from the authorities and sent it along with a statute and other papers. That is how the Svir Gymnastics Club became a legal institution as part of the Vilna Maccabee.

The Svir bicycle group of Ha'Poel - 1937

With the onset of autumn, the question of a Gymnastics-hall arose. At first, we rented a room from Lord Bakavitch on Dubelyaner Street. However, we could not use the equipment there. Later on, we moved to a larger room at Chaim Rabinovitch's where we installed the walls and used the bench. Finally, after my going to Vilna for the instruction course, the equipment was transferred to the Tarbut school.

Because of technical difficulties in conducting the Gymnastics work systematically, the Gymnastics club morphed into a football group.

The Mikhalishak youth was envious of the Svir sportsters and also founded a football group. After a period of training, they invited the Svir football players to come to them for a match.

Early one Saturday the Svir football players gathered at a certain point, and marched out of town in tight rows. They were brave, energetic and jolly.

The family of Berl Alperovitz

They did not even notice the more than 20 km they had traversed. Arriving at the bridge across the Vile near Mikhalishak, the bridge watchman came to us, and a little frightened, asked what was the meaning of the arrival of so many young men? After identifying ourselves, the watchman politely allowed us to cross the bridge. I then lined them up once more and the lusty youth marched into Mikhalishak

Despite the tiredness from so much walking, the Svir players, in front of many onlookers, smashed the Mikhalishak players.

After a gathering at which I stressed the meaning of physical education, they all returned to Svir.

Chaim, of blessed memory – Berl Alperovitz's father

The fame of the Svir football players spread far beyond the borders of our own town. After appropriate negotiations, the Sventsyon football players, under the leadership of the gymnastics teacher, Katcherginski, came to Svir. The news about this spread quickly throughout town, causing the youth to celebrate and eliciting astonishment from the older generation.

The eagerness surpassed all else. There were even those who showed complete understanding towards our youth and their games and the younger men and women even went to watch the battle between Svir and Sventsyon. Those who felt it was not proper to go, however did show some eagerness and inquired about what the news was from the "front". When the opposition returned from the Svir "war", the Svir people had the pleasure of knowing that Svir and Sventsyon had tied.

On May 25, 1924, a conference took place in Vilna for the purpose of spreading the idea of physical education in the province. At this conference, among other items, it was authorized that the first Jewish Gymnastics and Sport Club in the province of the Vilna area had been founded in Svir.

[Page 68]

The Svir Jewish Defense

by Dr. Ch. Swironi

Translated by Mindle Crystel Gross

Edited by Toby Bird z"l

In general, the Jews of Svir made an effort to live in friendly circumstances with their Christian neighbors, and this is the reason that many Svir residents had a place to hide during the time of the Nazis.

However, there were also many rabid anti-Semites, bandits and hooligans who were hired to create trouble for the Jews. The Jews were not afraid to stand up with strength to those Christians and to show them that a Jew also knows how to defend his honor.

The Christians in the entire area slowly recognized that it was not worthwhile to start up with Svir Jews.

One time, Christian boys from the Weistimer area came to Svir to report for induction. They brought a harmonica and got together in a chain formation and went around town, playing loudly, shouting and screaming that Jews must be beaten up.

They threw stones at windows, bothered passers-by, but they were unable to get as far as Pesakh Gabay's The Svir Jews organized and stood against them. Chaim Yisroel Kaganovitz, the tinsmith, came out with his son, Meyer. Yerakhmiyl Solamyak and his workers, Binyomin Kamin, Khanan Gendl and others brought clubs and taught the Christian boys a good lesson.

They quickly left town.

Another time, the youth demonstrated that it would not permit pogroms in Svir.

This happened when the Christian workers who repaired the bridge came every Sunday and Thursday. They carried on so that the Jews were actually afraid to venture out of their homes on these two days.

The youth organized, prepared iron and rubber clubs, and divided into groups: At the head of each group was a commander. They decided to defend themselves with all their strength.

One group was led by Yudl Gershovitz. His area was from Gitlin to Chaim Yisroel the tinsmith.

Shloyme Khadesh led a second group which was responsible for defending the houses from Chaim Yisroel to Eliyohu Moshe.

Shloyme Katz led a third group whose area was from Eliyohu Moshe to Ruven Chaim.

Yosef Khayt's group was to defend the market and Dubelyoner Street.

The bridge-workers left Meltsarek's restaurant which was then opposite Zalman the barber-surgeon's drugstore. A couple of boys were ordered to run away in order to draw the bridge-workers deep into the Jewish street.

And so it was – they pretended to run away and the bridge-workers chased after them. They drew them in almost to the market and there began the organized defense. Yosef Chaim immediately demonstrated that he was an outstanding tactician. The hooligans suddenly realized that they were surrounded on all sides. They called for help, but it was too late. Some Christians tried to help them, but they were not successful.

It was interesting that all the Christians from the so-called "Sloboda", or from Rumisher Street were on the side of the Jews.

The bridge-workers left town in shame and did not bother anyone again.

On Sundays and Thursdays, the Jews could once again walk in the street, free, and not be afraid of being stoned by a hooligan.

Slowly, the anti-Semites in the whole area recognized that Svir Jews could defend themselves, and that a group was organized here which can and wants to defend them, and it became peaceful in town, and up until the arrival of the Nazis, not one of them dared to attack us.

The Christians looked upon us Svir Jews with respect and honor and behaved honorably and friendly towards us.

[Page 71 - Yiddish]

The Svir Journals

By Herzl Weiner

Translated by Mindle Crystel Gross

Edited by Toby Bird z"l

The well-developed folk- library, the reading-room, the many daily newspapers, weekly journals and monthly publications, the frequent discussions and readings, the many-branched political activity, the very strong social pulse – all this had results. Not only was there discovered in Svir a circle of talented artists, but there also was a group of writers and literati.

The Svir literati group did not attempt to win any support anywhere else. They dedicated their entire energy in elevating the cultural level of their little town. They found a good method for this by publishing a weekly newspaper.

Between the two wars, the Svir literati group was able to publish several journals, the best of which were: *The Pakel* and *From Our Life*. Outstanding editors were both brothers Miller, Avrom Yitskhok and Henekh.

The following are examples of each of the Svir writers:

Poems by Avrom Yitskhok Miller

My Little Fiddle

I had a little fiddle,
Unusual, an antique,
And would often play a song
From famous works.

Many years passed.
I spent time with her alone.
My youth was lost in her,
In her sweet crying sounds.

Winter

Stars appear in the sky.
The day is passing by.
The street noise quiets,
As does the daily business.
The air is cold, one's nose freezes,
And still, it is pleasant to go.
The frost cuts as with steel,
And the eyes tear.
Shimmering, twinkling before the eyes,
Millions of snowflakes from afar,
And no matter how we turn our heads,
The snow shines all around.

Winter sport on the frozen lake

On a Clear Night

    The moon swims across the clear sky
    Surrounded by a million little stars.
    Quiet is the night, there is no wind.
    Everywhere dead, the earth silent.
    Everything is sunk in deep sleep.
    Only the moon moves about,
    But soon, even this will end,
    And the night is quickly over,
    With her secretive shine.
    Once again, the day will arrive
    With its wild devil-dance.

Politics

    The sun is burning.
    The world has now burst into bloom.
    I think that all is good and beautiful.
    We seed, we cut, we thresh, we plow,
    Only our world is – no evil should befall us –
    Large and broad, but with trouble.
    Wherever one goes, wherever one is,
    The sword is already prepared,
    And souls are trembling
    At the angry word "wars".

Only yesterday, we stood
And waited on the balconies
When, like roosters,
Angry, men looked at each other,
And after a while, probably
Another war would erupt.
A miracle, a dream happened,
And all passed, meanwhile, peacefully.

[Page 74]

Poems by Henekh Miller

1. Like a young pale widow
Who mourns her husband,
The moon swims languidly
In an easy, breezy fog.

2. The stars accompany her
On her far way
And they blink so nicely
And they dance without end.

Summer

1. The air is hot and suffused
With a sweet flowery aroma
Bright white clouds
Swimming on high.

2. Bent as if ashamed
Are the pretty branches
And dream like drunken
From the air.

3. Butterflies flit about
In the fields, on the air
And they dance and jump
Quite drunk with air.

4. It is also spring in the forest
Birds flit, sing, jump.
In the forest, the old king.
Reaps joy from the sounds.

5. At all of this with great pleasure
the sun looks down and shines,

and from the skies, the blue
rays spill down, spill down.

People

1. People rush and rush
For that small piece of bread.
They become confused because of this
Which was spread over the whole world.

2. People rush and rush,
For that little bit of good fortune.
Riches will not be had
To live lucky, without problems.

[Page 75]

A Poem by Khaye Kurtski

Loneliness

1. Life is lonely,
Like the death of the field.
Often he comes back
And finishes like a hero.

2. The years are lonely
And saturated with need
A person like he is born
To suffer for the smallest piece of bread.

3. Lonely is the hour
and every minute of life,
and all the troubles of the world
are all because of a false striving.

It is Difficult to Find

I know, my dear, that it is difficult for you,
So don't look for the truth, there is not much,
And should you ever find the truth,
Then you should know how dear it is,
And to care for and honor such a person
Who is as clean from falseness as a crystal.

Silent Tears

How bitter my tears may be,
I have swallowed them for many years.
No matter how difficult my life may be
I carry it quietly under my heart.
Painful was my youth
Without a bit of brightness and light.
I always dreamt, hoped,
Looked anxiously at the morrow, And then,
The morrow also passed,
And still no brightness or light.
Somewhere there is a beautiful world,
But mine is a dark one.

A Poem by Reyzl Khazan
(now Shoshana Drobkin)

You, too, came here,
To the choking air of injustice.
You say that it presses upon you, it is not good
To be among people who thirst for blood.
So don't be chosen from all others.
Be equal with all others
Who do endless things
The world suits you.

[Page 77]

A Poem by Sonia Tabarisk

The Dog

A dog barked, barked
From early morning until late at night,
Until he felt terrible,
And suddenly fell into deep thought
For a piece of a hard bone,
For a bone among the garbage,
It is not worthwhile to stand here
And bark unnecessarily.

The youth of Svir did not only express in these journals their feelings and thoughts, their dreams and strivings. All of the social, cultural, political and economic life in the town was reflected here. They wrote about everything and everything was discussed.

Naturally, what interested people the most were the questions of the youth. Henekh Miller devoted many articles to these problems. In *Our Life*, No 11, of July, 1923, he portrays, for example, the good qualities and desires of the Svir Jewish youth. This was following a literary *trial* about Mendele's text, which attracted all of the Svir youth, regardless of the differences in their beliefs and parties. Henekh Miller became interested in the feelings which the youth exhibited. In this article, he expresses his pleasure with the fact that the youth forgot their differences for at least one evening and united in satisfaction around a literary-drama circle.

**Henekh Miller and Malke Fisher,
of blessed memory**

Henekh Miller wrote, "that the literary *trial* refreshed the youth and brought in a sort of renewal of soul, a holiday atmosphere". At the end of the article, he appealed to all the young groups to strengthen the collective work, together to create, and this would be useful in all community institutions in Svir. In a second article, he speaks about the existence-question of the Jewish youth and reaches the interesting conclusion, that a professional school must be opened.

Ruven Meyer Reznik does not avoid the question of the speculative prizes. In an article with the meaningful title: *A Holiday for the Parasites*, he describes the scarcity of things in town and the rise in the cost of the prizes: "Hah, hah, it is lively, joyous, running, flitting about, whispering, a tumult, a commotion. What has happened? It is already almost a big deal, a holiday for the shopkeepers, an excitement, and a tragedy for the poor population."

Moshe & Rokhl-Leye Miller, of blessed memory and their family

In another article, Ruven Meyer addresses the question of the importance of noble descent to the Jews. He describes how a decent Jew is prepared to have his daughter marry an unemployed youth, one who relies on others for sustenance, one who is bankrupt, and even to one who is sick, anything not to enter into a family with no standing.

Avrum Yitskhok Miller, in a number of articles, tackles the problems of reading books. Like everybody else, he strives to read that which interests him, and is related to his feelings. Therefore the library must accommodate itself to the various preferences of its readers. For the youth, it is necessary to have romance novels and for the school children, travel books, discoveries and new developments.

Most importantly, he complains about the sad fact that in Svir very little Jewish history is taught.

He writes: "One is not a Jew without the history of the Jews. One is blind and dumb if one does not know Jewish history. Only with a Jewish heart, with Jewish sense and with Jewish nationalistic teachings. can he who studies Jewish history be a Jew".

He also believes that too few Hebrew books are being read.

Moshe Drevyatski writes an article about social institutions. He arrives at the correct conclusion that it is not a good thing that each group is involved only with itself, is self-absorbed and creates a sort of world unto itself.

Berl Alperovitz writes very interesting articles. Naturally, he is consumed with sports questions. Once, in 1923, there was a football match between the Svir and Sventsyon players, which ended with the official score of 0-1 in favor of Sventsyon. He came out against them, and claims that the result was an unfair one, that the Sventsyon players, according to his opinion, did not deserve their goal.

"The 11 meter kick was given and the ball was returned back by the Svir gatekeeper, but the ball was immediately, once again, kicked by one of the Sventsyon player who was in the penalty field. This is not permitted. With an 11 meter kick, nobody except the kicker is allowed to be in the penalty field".

Since the Sventsyon players triumphed and shouted three times Hurrah, Berl Alperovitz

gives this example" "Once upon a time, somebody went to the ritual slaughterer and asked him to kill his geese. The slaughterer asks him how many geese he had, and it turns out that in total, only one goose, and she is already dead".

On the lake in 1933

Alperovitz concludes his article:

"Certainly the Sventsyon football players will also talk about the goals which they gave to Svir, but if one should ask them how many goals they gave, they will also have to answer "a dead one", a false one".

In three separate articles, Avrum Yitskhok Miller describes the football match between Svir and Mikhalishak. He describes how the Svir players came Friday evening on foot, almost to Mikhalishak, how they crossed the deep river and rested in the forest. He describes the welcome in Mikhalishak, and above all, Svir's great victory

Before the match, Berl Alperovitz made an important speech about the physical development of the Jewish youth and at the end, stressed the necessity of establishing a tournament and sport club in Mikhalishak as well.

Henekh Miller always wrote about sports in every newspaper.

A number of articles by Alikim Kovarski were directed to questions about music and cantorial music.

The teacher, Chaim Rogov, wrote an interesting article called *Shehkhiyonu,* in which he greets the founder of the Zionist Socialist youth organization.

It is interesting that from all the newspapers we received, we learned that Shloyme Khetser had presented a talk about Morris Rosenfeld and Yakov Dov Gordon. The rabbi's son-in-law spoke about the Hebrew literature and the *Tanakh,* Chaim Rogov gave lessons about cultural history.

An interesting announcement was made public on January 20, 1924:

> Do you want to enjoy an evening?
> Do you want to benefit from one evening?
> Come Saturday evening, to family night
> A program of enriching content
> Buffet and entertainment
> Come all.

In short, everybody who looks through the newspapers and their many editions which appear in Svir, must be astonished and wonder at the courage and energy and enthusiasm which the Svir youth had.

In the 20th edition of *From Our Life*, the editor published an article with the headline *20 Editions.*

He writes therein:

"With much happiness and pleasure, we are publishing the 20th edition of *From Our Life*. We have covered a lot of ground under very difficult and terrible circumstances. These 20 editions demonstrate on what level the youth of Svir stands, relative to culture and development".

However, poetry did not appear daily. The most important reason was that when the most talented left in later years, younger talents appeared in the journals, such as Hertsl Viner, Khanon Viner, Ekhad Miller, Dovid Hayt, Shmuel Dobkin, Yosef Zlatayavke and many other friends, boys and girls.

Jewish youth near the Memorial on the hill

Modest and without pretensions, they all influenced and created, and all those who remained alive may to this very day, be proud along with their friends with whom for tens of years they were fortunate enough to become educated and work together for the good of their little town.

[Page 85]

Chapter Three

Terrible Events

[Page 87]

Avremele Yoel

by Chanoch Drutz

Translated by Mindle Crystel Gross

Edited by Toby Bird z"l

Svir Jews lived through many tragedies during the period between the two wars, but not one of them was as traumatic as Avremele's death.

A handsome, young, energetic and serious youth appears before everyone's eyes up to this very day, and when the rabbi, in his funeral oration compared him to a young, strong and rooted tree which was cut down in the middle of blooming, he described precisely what everyone was thinking.

Already as a small boy, Avremele had the reputation of a clever child, quick-witted and talented,. He was one of the top students in school and as a child, was known to be a true and devoted friend. He was friendly to everyone, and most importantly, he liked to do favors.

Townspeople would speak with great enthusiasm about his good character. He dedicated his entire youthful energy to organizing the youth of Svir. He was the important soul of the *khalutz* and *frayhay* (Freedom) movements, so it was really no wonder that his tragic death affected the residents of Svir in every aspect of their world like a thunder-clap and nobody could find relief from his sorrow and pain.

In addition, this tragedy struck exactly two weeks after his eldest brother, Berl, left for Eretz Yisroel. Avremele, too, dreamt about Eretz Yisroel, and through Berl he even sent his belongings there because in case he would have to make aliya illegally, he thought it would be better for him to travel with less baggage.

[Page 88]

On Wednesday, November 21st, 1934, around five p.m., Avremele and Zalman Borukh were preparing, as always, for the Thursday market. On that day, Avremele was in a hurry because that evening he was to go to a meeting of the *He'khalutz Ha-tsair*.

Since it was already quite dark, they lit a lantern and set out with a pail to the storehouse to fill it with benzene. This was their usual method of preparation for market-day.

However, it was already very dark in the storehouse. The lantern was on the side with neither of them noticing that the pail was already full. Avremele picked up the lantern and walked over close to the pail in order to check if it was full. A spray of benzene hit him. The pail caught fire and the flame found Avremele.

On fire, he ran into the street in the direction of the market, across the street from the doctor. He managed to run as far as the pharmacy of Israel Gordon, which was, at that time, in the house of Pesye Svirski.

This entire time, people saw that a fireball was running, but they did not realize what this meant. Finally, when he reached the pharmacy, they threw him to the ground, covered him with clothing, and after putting the fire out, they carried him into the pharmacy where he lay for five hours.

Meanwhile, it became evident that also Zalman Borukh had been burned, but not as badly – only his face and hands. But he also had terrible pains, screamed, gnashed his teeth and pulled out his hair.

Those who were helping the wounded, sent for a taxi from Sventsyon, which did not arrive until 12 midnight. They then took the two wounded to the *Guardian of the Sick Hospital* in Vilna.

[Page 89]

Avremele Yoel, of blessed memory

Dr. Salkindson, who took charge of them, immediately confirmed that Avremele's condition was very grave, because three-quarters of his body had been burned. And yet, he was totally conscious the entire time. He answered all questions with precision, but did not realize how grim his condition was.

Since a number of Svir *khalutzim* were at that time in Vilna for training, they were reached by telephone and quickly the cousins Nosn and Yosef Chaim came to the bedsides of both Avremele and Zalman Borukh.

It became evident that Avremele's condition was hopeless. Zalman Borukh was moved from the room he shared with Avremele so he would not witness the passing of his beloved younger brother.

[Page 90]

On Thursday, the 22nd of November, around 1 p.m., Avremele Yoel, the heroic, handsome youth, the pride of Svir, passed away in the hospital in Vilna.

A short while after, Nosn telephoned his brothers in Svir, informing them that Avremele was no longer with them, and that Gitl must be prepared to learn this.

Her sorrow and pain were difficult to witness, but she gave no thought to death. She still believed that he would be saved and she decided that evening to travel to Vilna early Friday morning.

Nothing her sisters said could persuade her to wait. She remained stubborn, that she must see the children. Meanwhile, Yosef telephoned that they would bring him, Avremele, around 10 p.m. Everyone became confused. They did not know what to do with Gitl. They quickly held a consultation and they decided to escort her to Tsirl's and the deceased would be taken there as well.

Nine o'clock in the evening, when once again, she began to say that she wanted to go to Vilna, Tsirl tearfully told her that there was no reason for her to go to Vilna, that they were bringing him here. She now realized how huge this tragedy was.

The wailing and crying in the entire town cast a pall of unequaled sorrow.

When at 10 p.m. the taxi carrying the deceased arrived at Tsirl's doorstep, hundreds of people broke into mournful cries.

The funeral

The active members of *He'khalutz* consulted the entire night about how to handle the funeral. All the details were worked out, and at 9 a.m., the funeral procession began from Tsirl's house.

[Page 91]

At the fresh grave of Avremele Yoel, of blessed memory. November 1934

They came by the hundreds to pay their last respects to their tragically deceased friend and to accompany him on his final way.

When the *khalutzim* began to move with the casket, all imagined that even the stones of the bridge also wept.

All the various organizations were represented.

The huge line of mourners stretched to Zelig Svirski's house, and continued in the direction of the synagogue. There it halted, and Rabbi Berkman gave the funeral oration.

They continued on to the premises of the *Hehalutz* where Chanoch Miller spoke about him. Slowly, the long mournful line continued on to the cemetery, and although it was a cold November day, no one left.

[Page 92]

Hertzl Weiner, Dovid Chaim and cousin Berl all spoke at the open grave. Everyone expressed his sorrow at the great loss to the youth of Svir, when in a horrible and tragic manner, one of their own was torn away, one of the best and most devoted friends. He was a friend who strived his entire life to make aliya to Eretz Yisroel and suddenly, he passed away before his wish could be realized.

The crowd dispersed about 2 p.m.

There was sorrow in town Friday evening. We heard no conversation, all gatherings and meetings were cancelled.

The sorrow after the funeral

After shiva, a week later, Saturday evening, at the premises of the *He'khalutz* there took place a sorrow counseling session. They had enlarged Avremele's photo and placed it near the table where sat the speakers. All of the youth of Svir participated, regardless of their party differences and affiliations because Avremele was beloved and dear to everyone. Gitl and Tsirl were also present.

The session opened with a march of sorrow. Hertzl Weiner opened the proceedings. Chanoch Miller spoke in the name of *Hehalutz*, Shmuel Reznik in the name of the *gmilas khesed* (The Benevolent Loan Society), Abba Weiner in the name of *Ha'oved* (youth organization). Everyone described the terrible loss that their little Jewish town had sustained.

After the *shloshim* (30 days of mourning), the *Hehalutz* published a brochure about his life and his accomplishments. It was put together by Chanoch Miller and Hertzl Weiner.

On Saturday, December 15th, there was a general gathering where it was decided to build a community center in his name. A committee was elected: Yisroel Gordon, Moyshe Drevyatski, Shmuel Svirski, Yosef Zlatayavke, Moyshe Miller and Berl Reznik. The concern regarding a second world war, however, did not permit the realization of this plan.

[Page 93]

And yet, they printed the publication which the committee put together and mailed it to the residents of Svir living in Eretz Israel.

The appeal

On Monday, November 21st, 1934, at 5 p.m., a fire broke out in Svir which took the life of one of our best, Friend Avrom Yoel, who died tragically in flames.

The town was shattered by this tragedy. Death took away from us forever one of our best friends, one of the first initiators in the organizing of the youth in the preparation of the building of Eretz Israel.

Our tragically deceased friend strived to witness the realization of this ideal, to be one link in the entire chain of building a viable Eretz Israel.

We find it necessary, thanks to his fund-raising in the name of the building-up of Eretz Yisroel, to build a community center in the Diaspora, but the community center will be the place where we will be able to spin the thread of many long generations with you, our friends, in Eretz Israel. To make this plan an actuality is, however, associated with material difficulties. Therefore, we appeal to you, friends, to help us realize our plan. We turn to you, our friends, because you are the only ones who will understand the necessity for such a center, which will provide the possibility of educating our youth in the spirit of a functioning Eretz Israel.

This action has already begun. We have already received contributions through arranged evening events, etc.

[Page 94]

Velvl (Zev) Yoel, of blessed memory

We distributed this announcement and everything is being carried out with the greatest expenditure of energy and money.

Friends, respect the value of our work and help by placing a brick in the building in the name of the tragically deceased Avremel Yoel, of blessed memory.

Histadrut Hehalutz in Poland
Svir Branch

It was in this way that Svir mourned one of its best and dearest children.

Up to this very day, Avremele Yoel, of blessed memory, still appears alive before everyone's eyes, and no one, no one has forgotten him nor will forget him.
May his memory be forever blessed!

[Page 95]

Misfortune in the *Hachshara*
[training for pioneers to *Eretz-Yisroel*].

Translated by Mindle Crystel Gross

Edited by Toby Bird z"l

As everywhere else, the Svir *halutzim* took upon themselves various work responsibilities in order to prepare for their aliya. Sometimes this work was in town and other times, in an out-of-town *kibbutz*.

Once, the Svir *Hehalutz* accepted work in a farm, where a machine was cutting straw. Working there among others was Eliyahu Kamin. He did not notice that his sleeve had gotten caught in the machine. In the blink of an eye, four fingers of the left hand were cut off. The other *halutzim* brought him home and the surgeon-barber, Margevitz, bandaged his hand. In the morning, they took him to Vilna.

For the first few weeks, Eliyahu Kamin was very frightened, but later on, was able to think more rationally and began to think of his future. After his wounds healed, he took a course in bookkeeping, and got work in an iron business in Vilna at the corner of Zavalne and Troker Streets.

Even more terrible and more frightening was a second incident with the Svir *khalutzim* who were in a Vilna *kibbutz* in Subatch.

This happened in 1936. *Khalutzim* were working in a clay factory. The work consisted of grinding the bones of cows which would then be made into clay.

[Page 96]

Berl Dimentshteyn was standing near the machine and noticed that a bone was stuck, halting the machine. Instead of turning the machine off, and removing the bone, he inserted his hand, trying to pull the bone out. However, the machine began to work and pulled him in.

**Berl Dimentshteyn,
of blessed memory**

It chopped his head off right to his shoulders, Yitskhok Mikhnavitch immediately fainted when he witnessed the cut-up body.

This tragedy occurred December 12th, and made a terrible impression on the entire population of Vilna. For an entire night the casket remained and thousands of people walked around it. An honor guard stood in attendance until the funeral.

The funeral took place the following day around 12 noon, with almost the entire youth population of Vilna participating since it was a weekday. They used sleds to get to the cemetery.

[Page 97]

Special representatives from *He'khalutz* in Warsaw attended. All the newspapers in Vilna printed notices about this incident. Workers left their jobs, merchants closed their businesses. The entire town was engulfed in sorrow. In all the *kibbutzim* in Poland, there took place grief counseling.

At the end of the 30 day mourning period, a huge gathering was held. When Berl's mother came and saw the large photo, she fell into a faint.

**Khalutzim honor guard at the
casket of Berele Dimentshteyn, of blessed memory**

On December 12th, 1937 the first anniversary of his death, the *Hehalutz* of Vilna erected a headstone at the grave of the unfortunate Dimentshteyn in the form of a truncated birch tree.

The Vilna *khalutzim* issued a special brochure dedicated to his memory in which Hertzl Weiner wrote about him.

In his poem, Hertzl related how the young Dimentshteyn dreamt about making aliya to Eretz Yisroel and to become part of the thousands of builders. He compared him to a young twig which quickly died.

[Page 98]

And so our blossoming life vanished, and to the list of the youth of Svir martyrs were added more victims.

Honor the *khalutz* who fell before his dream was realized.

[Page 99]

Chapter Four
Memories

[Page 101]

Memories of a *Kheder-Yingl*
[religious primary school boy]

by Aharon Koury

Translated by Mindle Crystel Gross

Edited by Toby Bird z"l

The onset of spring was dear to every Jewish boy, most especially when we had been imprisoned the entire winter from early morning until into the night in a cramped room with half a score other children, with a strict rabbi, and with stale air which turned a boy's brain dull and lazy.

I was at that time a boy of about eight or nine, and springtime was sweet and dear. First of all, the door to the room remained open and fresh, clean, soft air came in. In the morning, my mother gave us a delicious dairy breakfast.

The ice from the frozen river melted and the broad, white area of huge distances disappeared between our houses. Once again, the water began to flow freely and a new world opened up before our eyes. Once more, we could roll up our pants, jump into the water, and fill a pail with water for our mother. At the edge could be seen tiny little fish in the thousands swimming back and forth. To this very day, I don't know of any other place where there are so many little fish as there were in the Svir River.

So therefore, it is no wonder that early in the morning I ran out of the house and breathed in the refreshing air.

The water in the river was like a beautiful, clear mirror. The sun shone from every side of the river with all her glory and beauty; the horizon was gorgeous.

[Page 102]

From the right side where the waves originated, one could hear quite clearly when a fisherman's line hit the water. The echo was loud and measured. Everything would seem to melt into one wonderful panorama.

I stood there, dreamily, mesmerized, at the edge of the river, until I heard my mother's shout:

Why are you standing there like a statue and dreaming?

Then I went back, not to the house, but to the garden. We had planted potatoes, beets, carrots, beans, cucumbers and other greens. The garden caused my mother much aggravation and also much effort and work. My brother and I helped her cheerfully.

We were pleased that the winter had already gone and we could open the double windows which, for half the year, were locked, sealed and stuffed with cotton. Now we could feel in the kheder the aroma of all that was blooming in the garden, and we could study Torah with enthusiasm.

From then on, boyish years passed like this, and to this day, we cannot forget this. I imagine the mirror on the Svir River mesmerized me, and caused me more wonder than the most beautiful and wonderful symphony.

Toiling Jews

by Matityahu Bogdanov

Translated by Mindle Crystel Gross

Edited by Toby Bird z"l

The synagogue had one door which was the entrance, but there were also three other doors – one on the left, to the north, which was the door to the small synagogue (kloyz), a second to the right, to the south, which led to the entrance to the women's synagogue.

[Page 103]

A little distance from the second door, there was a third upon which was written: *The trustees are here from 11 to 12*. This indicated that this was the door behind which were collected various items that poor Jews brought in as collateral against the loans which they had taken from the *gmilat hesed* (Loan Society).

Velvl the Blacksmith, of blessed memory

As a young boy, I liked to peer in through the door of the society which carried the name of *gmilat hesed*. Rabbi Meyer Fayvishes (Zlatayavka), who was one of the trustees, would open the heavy lock, remove the iron bar, and when he opened the door, I, having pg. 104 hidden, would look at the household articles which lay there: wagon-wheels, a saddle with reins, brass candlesticks, samovars, clothing and many other items which Jews used to pawn when they needed a few rubles to pay a fine or to pay tuition or when someone needed something for the Sabbath.

The two doors which were opposite one another – the small synagogue door and the *gmilas khesed* door had a particular connection, because most clients of the *gmilas khesed* were those who prayed in the small synagogue. As I recall and as they remain in my memory, they were *the small synagogue Jews*. Those Jews, were honest, hard-working artisans, village merchants and so forth. There were not many scholars among them and therefore, they felt in the small synagogue, as if they were in their own homes. Here they lived their spiritual lives, each in his way. If one could read *mishne* – all the better – if not, they made do with a chapter of psalms, a portion of *khumash*.

However, they did have Arbin, a great scholar who loved the plain folk. He studied the portion of the week with them and a little bit of the stories of the *Talmud*. Their rabbi was Rabbi Yekhiel Mordekhay, the fur merchant.

Among these small synagogue Jews, there were those who had a weakness for the pulpit.

I remember the competition which went on between Bentsye the Shoemaker and Moshe-Leyb the Tailor for a Sabbath *minkha* service. Both virtually ran to the pulpit and whoever got there first was the one to pray there.

I remember that Moshe-Leyzer's *minkha* praying at the pulpit was so famous that his grandson, with whom I was in heder, we used to call by the name of a prayer, as a nickname.

Here in the small synagogue, the worshippers also had an opportunity to receive an *aliya*

(honor) sometimes which they would seldom receive in the large synagogue. Pg. 105 Among the small synagogue Jews, there were also some who sacrificed their lives for a *mitzvah* (good deed) such as visiting the sick, Talmud Torah or helping a poor bride. Yankl the Shoemaker would wake up at 3 a.m. during the winter, had already tucking the left arm of his coat into his belt, ready to lay *tfillin* (phylacteries), and this was how he would slowly make a few upper soles.. This man, Yankl, could spend entire nights at the bedside of someone who was sick so as to give the family members a chance to rest.

And if a horse that belonged to one of the small synagogue Jews died, with kerchief in hand, they went around to collect several rubl, going among their own class, and the Jew who had lost his horse would be able to buy another horse in order to earn a living.

May my few sentences be as a monument for those Jews whom I have described herein, and to those among them who fell as victims of Hitlerism. May God take revenge for their shortened lives.

Memories of Svir

by Ben-Tzion Gold

Translated by Mindle Crystel Gross

Edited by Toby Bird z"l

Our Svir citizens in Israel approached the landslayt in America asking them to submit in writing their memories for the book *Our Little Town of Svir* which was been compiled by our Dr. Chanoch Drutz-Sviruni, with help from Svir landslayt in Israel who submitted material, facts and stories.

At first, I removed myself from those who were able to contribute to the book. In order to write something, I must take into consideration that as soon as I imagine the town, the first thoughts I have are of my acquaintances who perished at the hands of the murderous Nazis either in Svir or in the concentration camps.

[Page 106]

**Sore Rivke Fisher,
of blessed memory**

 I thought about this for a long time, and then I realized that my writing would be like the words on a headstone which do not need any preparation or agreement. Years later, when Svir will be no more than a name and someone from a later generation of Svir descendants will want to peer into this book, he will absorb from my words something which will help him to reach a better understanding of his ancestral town.

 Lately, books have been published, memories of a number of cities and towns which, like Svir, were destroyed during WWII. One can see in all of them that the life was uniquely Jewish and had many genteel and learned Jews. I think that Svir was different from the other towns. The reputation that Svir was a learned town is truly correct, but maybe not to great scholarly depth or with a large number, but in comparison with those other towns, they were on a higher level. But in Svir, among the learned, there were fur merchants, butchers, bakers, tailors. Such a democratic collection was, at that time, unusual.

[Page 107]

**Chanoch and Kayle Gelger with their daughters
& On the right Zisl and Malke Alperovitz**

The decent learned atmosphere in Svir was tolerated by the opposing workers' groups and Zionists. Sometimes incidents did occur which were neither frequent nor serious. Certainly the bosses could not tolerate an agitator from a larger city coming to Svir, finding a captive audience in the synagogue and forcing everyone to listen to an agitation-speech of his party.

[Page 108]

The decent Jews tolerated other groups, but they most certainly did not think too much of them, not even of the Zionists who were ideologically not too different from the bosses. I remember that one time after morning services (shakhrit), there began a debate about Zionism. One, an elderly Jew, made a remark that Dr. Herzl, of blessed memory, has earned as great a place in heaven as Moses. Well, that was all he needed. The word *heretic* which they called him was not among the strongest used.

**Lolye Zlatavyavka, of blessed memory,
selling newspapers during WWI**

During the inter-war years, a remarkable change occurred in the education and development of the young generation. Lately, I had the opportunity to meet with people from Svir of the younger generation, and I was amazed at their worldliness and modern outlook at life. One must not take from this that the new generation is spiritually on a higher plane than the previous generation. We must only marvel at the differences which are almost unbelievable, that it happened in so short a time.

[Page 109]

We from Svir in America, are very thankful to our landslayt in Israel for their great devotion in gathering the material for the book. A separate thank-you is due he who compiled it all, our beloved landsman, Dr. Chanoch Drutz, without his great effort, the book would not have been realized, and there would not be a lasting memory of Svir. With the publication of the book, there remains with us from Svir the spiritual connection with the town of our birth. The book is even dearer to us because it is written in wonderful Yiddish, virtually in every word – holy, and evokes memories which will always remain within us.

With everyone's permission, I want to mention the names of my closest, whose graves I will never see: my grandfather and grandmother, R'Yitskhok-Yankev and Zlate Lifshitz; my parents, R'Borukh-Ber and Malke-Tsive Zlatayavka; my brothers Eliyohu and his wife, Yisroel (Lolye) and his daughters; my sisters Grunye and her daughter Zlate and Sonye and her family; my mother-in-law Sore Rivke Fisher; my brother-in-law Zisl and his family and my sister-in-law Kayle Gelgar and her family.

[Page 110]

Remembrances of Svir

by Joe Salav

Translated by Mindle Crystel Gross

Edited by Toby Bird z"l

A town in the length, little streets,
A street with beautiful gardens,
A hospital, even a church,
A wooden bridge not far away,
Which would have fallen in a long time ago
Were it not for ropes.

A mountain which protects us from enemies
Upon which we used to climb
When we were children.
We used to play, galloping in the valleys
On the mountain – up and down.

Do you remember the river where the children used to swim?
Do you remember the gardens where flowers bloomed?
Do you remember the lake where the children used to bathe?
Did not keep all this on

We did not keep our clothes on
We used to spray ourselves
And afterwards make the spray
Go all over, and we laughed joyously.

My landslayt, do you remember
When we left kheder
At night, with lanterns, with shouts and song,
And from the broad, deep swamp,
We would barely make it home.

[Page 111]

Do you remember the synagogue, do you remember the small synagogue?
Do you remember our kheder in the little old house
Where we all studied from morning until late at night?
And not one of us became a rabbi.

Now, who knows what became
Of our once-upon-a-time town where we were born.
The few landslayt who remained there
Were murdered by Hitler, annihilated.

My Birthplace

Shoshana Drapkin

Translated by Sara Mages

I know about Svir less than all the Svir people, and I remember the early days as through a fog, because I was five years old when we moved from the place where we lived.

I only remember that when we left Svir they sat me and my brother of blessed memory inside a cupboard on a pile of pillows, either from lack of space or from fear of rain. In this manner we traveled about forty kilometers to the city of Smorgon, and returned to Svir a few years later, in 1922. The neighbors, who shared their home with us, received us very well and prepared a room for me. The rest of the family lived with my aunt. I had the feeling that I fell from heaven to earth.

That very evening I met almost all the town's youth. At first, these "well-to-do loafers" left a very bad impression on me. Ignorant, I thought in my heart, and indeed, none of them had a profession and none of them worked. All of them still lived with their parents. But soon I realized that in the library, which was quite rich, there was not an unread book. Over time they started to laugh at my Yiddish which was mixed with Russian words. This prompted me to read all the books in Yiddish.

[Page 112]

Shabtai Hazan and his wife of blessed memory

My influence on them was valuable and in the course of time, the house that served as a center for the idle youth, emptied out. There were four sisters in this house but only two of them stood out: the youngest, a smart developed girl, tended to Zionism, and the second, an older one, was a typical "*Bund*" member. This house served as a youth center for thinkers, and every conversation led to a heated debate. But slowly they moved to a more productive work and a "*Halutz*" chapter was founded. Also the "*Tzeirei Zion*" council was very active: they had frequent lectures and social dances. We published the booklet "Our lives", and almost everyone participated. In 1924, two and a half months after the establishment of "*HeHalutz*", I traveled with another council member to Israel. We were the first to immigrate.

[Page 113]

At first, there was a strong connection with the town and we aroused great interest. Young women also joined the "*Halutz*" movement, prior to that I was the only female member. The youth awakened to intellectual life and left to study at the universities. Some started to immigrate to Israel, but of course, the majority, like anywhere in the Diaspora, remained and was caught by the wicked oppressor.

May their memory be blessed, we will remember them forever.

From the days of my childhood

Arye Gur-Arye (Pekel)

Translated by Sara Mages

After all, who is not familiar with the "Svirer Mountain?" Except for its pedigree, which originated in the days of Napoleon, it was well known in the whole area. Don't you remember the famous "blessing" "may you become swollen like the Svirer Mountain?" And who enjoyed the "Svirer Mountain?"- the Jews and the Gentiles alike.

The Lake. The lake, known as the "Svirer pond," falls to the "Reke" whose water does not freeze in the summer and in the winter. This lake played an important role in Svir's economic life. The Svirer fishermen were famous in the region, and Jews and non- Jews reached Greater Vilna with their fish. The fish, especially the "Yazge", called "the Svirer Yazge," were famous in the area. It is a small fish, from which the women of Svir learned to prepare delicacies.

Around the mountain and on the lakeshore huts and houses stood. Among them wooden houses and brick houses, covered with tiles or with straw. A road, paved with big stones, crossed between the houses. In our time there were no sidewalks on both sides of the street – this was Svir.

There was not one street in Svir. There were a number of streets: The Fishermen's Street, Eli Natans Street, and Yudah Velvele's Lane with its great slope. There was also the Beit Hamidrash Street (the synagogue courtyard). All of them stretched in the direction of the lake. There was another street, which was called "The Slobode Street". The Starovery [old believers] lived there.

[Page 114]

They were muscular men with oversize beards. Their "Tserkva" [church] stood at the end of the street. There were also streets that led to the mountain, among them was Avremale the chimney cleaner's Street.

There were two squares in Svir. They stood desolated all the days of the week. Sometimes, we practiced soccer there (there was a soccer field next to the Christian cemetery). But on Thursday, market day, the squares were full of people. One served as a "horse market" and the second as a "grain market".

On the slope, by the lakeshore, proudly stood the building of the Beit Hamidrash, it was taller than the huts around it. Next to it was the public bathhouse on one side and the poorhouse on the other side.

On the lakeshore, not far from Beit Hamidrash, fenced on all sides, was a lonely small house with patched windows. This house was a world in itself. And in this house, in a dungeon, was "R'Burech's *Heder*".

I was seven when my father, may he rest in peace, brought me to this house. It was the day after *"Shabbat Bereishit"* [The Shabbat after Simchat Torah]. The wintry weather brought darkness to the house. My father introduced me to R'Baruch. Before me stood a strong man, with broad shoulders and a trimmed beard. He held a "pointer" in his right hand. He wore a hat and a sweater without a coat. I looked at the house. It was a small room, four by four. There were tables next the three walls, and children sat around them and studied aloud.

After a few questions of "getting acquainted", such as: Where are you from boy? What is your name? What did you learn? Who was your rabbi? and so on – he pointed to a space between two boys, and with that I was added to the class.

I studied ten "periods" with R'Baruch, and graduated when I turned twelve. I must thank this man. He was the first to teach grammar from Mordechai Bezalel Schneider's book. He wrote the rules and we copied them. I still remember the melody and the rules of "the little lines and the little dots…" or the various Hebrew conjugations. I still remember the slaps that I received from his strong hand when I did not pronounce the words correctly. Although I was angry then and I also cried, I now know that he was the one who planted the love in my heart for beautiful Hebrew and correct pronunciation.

[Page 115]

No wonder that his students led the war for a Hebrew "Tarbut" School in Svir. And no wonder that his students were the first to immigrate to Israel.

The **Beit Hamidrash** was a large wooden building with a "women's gallery" upstairs and a "vestibule" downstairs. The *Bimah* stood in the middle and a table covered with a colorful tablecloth stood on it. The *Shamash* pounded on this table and announced *"Ya'ale Veyavo"* ["rise and come" – a prayer recited on the first day of the Jewish month and on holidays] and *"Tal Umatar"* [the prayer for rain]. Various preachers and speakers spoke from this *Bimah* about current affairs.

Here, I heard R'Yossi of blessed memory, the iron and hardware dealer, praying *"Kabbalat Shabbat"* [the receiving of the Shabbat]. With his enthusiasm he put out the lit candles on the "amud" [the cantor's stand]. Here I also heard the prayer of R'Feitel. His prayer was different from the prayer of R'Yossi. R'Yossi was shouting, demanding and protesting the injustice that was inflicted on God's nation. R'Feitel was not like that. He stood by the cantor's stand, his Tallit dropping over his narrow shoulders, and with his quite clear voice he asked and begged. The congregation saw clearly that his prayer was rising to the heavens and was received before the Creator. He always prayed quietly, and his serenity penetrated the heart. Only once I heard him raising his voice, it was during the prayer *"Hineni Heani Mima'as"* [Here I stand before thee]. The old man pleaded before his Creator that his prayer be accepted, "whose beard is fully grown, whose voice is sweet," and whispered *"Yehi Ratzon"* [may it be your will]. It was quiet in the synagogue. The congregation was poised for his special *"Yitgaddal veyitkaddash"* [May His great name be exalted and sanctified]. And here, the old man stood erect like a lion, and shouted "May you denounce the Satan, that he not impede me". This was his only shout during the prayer, but all of us saw, beyond a shadow of a doubt, that the "Angel of Death" covered its face with its wing and left. The old man defeated the prosecutor. Satan could not withstand the prayer of R'Feitel.

There were Jews in Svir who gathered in the synagogue every evening, "between *Mincha* and *Maariv*", and studied together around a table. They had a special table. There was another table in the synagogue where Jews, who couldn't "study on their own," sat. Here sat a Jew and read to them: *"Halachot"* [Jewish laws], *"Chayei Adam"* [the Life of Man] and *"Ein Yaakov"*. Around him sat the laborers, who came after a hard day of work, to hear "a sacred word".

[Page 116]

I was thirteen when I left Svir and went to study in Greater Vilna. Since then, I rarely visited Svir. Over time, the town developed and youth federations were established - *"HeHalutz"* and *"HaOved"*. Many immigrated to Israel and participated in the building of the country. Former residents of Svir are among those who fell in the War of Independence. Some emigrated overseas, and the rest? the rest? – where are you the Yossis and the Feitels, where do you study *"Gemara"* and *"Ein Yaakov"*? Where are you the "Psalms readers" with R'Bentze the shoemaker in the lead? Where are you the members of *"HeHalutz"*, *"HaOved"*, and the rest of the federations who lost their chance to go to Eretz Israel? Nobody knows where you are buried, and a memorial was not erected on your graves. May these words be a remote cornerstone to the memorial that will be built by those who cherish your names, so future generations will know that there was a Jewish community in the town of Svir, Poland.

The mountain is standing, the river is flowing and continues to provide its fish, but the Jews, our beloved Jews – are gone.

May their souls be bound in the bond of everlasting life.

[Page 117]

Chapter Five

The Destruction of Svir

[Page 119]

A Memorial Candle

Shmuel Dobkin

Translated by Yocheved Klausner

Silently I am standing before the written memorial – an eternal monument in memory of our town Svir, our cradle on foreign soil, the town that was destroyed and is not any more.

My heart is shivering and aching. My eyes are in tears and there are no words that I can speak. Human lips are too weak to express the full depth of pain and sorrow.

With trembling hands, with a feeling of holiness I now light an eternal candle to the memory of the dwellings of my childhood – this treasured corner of the world that radiated light and warmth and parents' love – an eternal love that was ruined and forever sealed off. And to the memory of our dear parents whose heart was always awake and apprehensive for every one of us, who were tortured with terrible cruelty in a desecrated land and returned their souls to Heaven in holiness and purity.

And to the memory of our sisters, gentle and loving in life, who did not part in death – who drank the cup of bitterness to the end and died somewhere in the death-camps, alone and forsaken.

And to the memory of our brothers, working and striving, honest and righteous, gentle souls who were burned alive and their pure souls rose to Heaven in flames. And to the memory of all the members of our family who have perished in the valley of slaughter. The tall and many-branched trees have been cut down and uprooted. Our heart, our heart aches for you, dear and beloved, who can replace you in our hearts?

We shall carry with love their holy memory in our grieving hearts and we shall never forget them. May these words be a memorial candle to their souls.

Yitgadal Veyitkadash…

[Page 120]

Destruction and Revenge

Poems by Fanye Fisher

Translated by Mindle Crystel Gross

Edited by Toby Bird z"l

My Little Town Svir

My little town Svir,
How I yearn for you
That was so dear and loved
Every street, every house
Where I cried and laughed
Spent my best years there
Spun sweet dreams
Lived through joy and suffering
There
In my small house
Little children played
Charming, pretty
Svir River, rich with fish
Many families benefited
The town adorned
Our youth – strolling
No problems, no worries
Thinking of nothing
With laughter, song
Spent time on the water
Svir mountain, tall and proud
Covered in flowers
Its entire breadth
Opened before our eyes
My little town, my home
You are for me today
Lost ,dead
What happened?
I will see you no more
The same sky, the same earth
But the Jewish people are missing
Every tree of my home.

Every stone of my street
Is a witness to German
Wildness and hate
Destroyed our home
The Jewish people
Murdered, burned
My little town, my former home
A lost dream.

[Page 121]

Chaim Meltzer, his bride Zlate Fisher

[Page 122]

The Memorial

The fifth of April, akh, terrible day
How big is my tragedy
How deep my sadness, my lamentation
The memorial candles, the silent witnesses
They burn, melt
Cry over my children, they help
How I envy my mother
Who left along with her children
I was not as fortunate
I must struggle in this world
The murderers spilled the blood of children
The Jewish mother was punished
Akh, God, where is Your justice
Your true justice?
You cut down the little ones
Let the slaughterers remain
My poem is not poetic, fine
But it is spun
With anguish and pain
There is nothing left of my children
Nothing, not a grave.

In Hiding

Be quiet, my child, my crown
Your crying will not help
The murderers will not understand us anyway
Be strong, my child
Just wait until the night passes
Don't cry, child
The night will end
The morning will be good

[Page 123]

The child choked from hunger
Held close to my heart
His face pale
His eyes dull
All night
The mother is awake
She no longer feels fear
No hunger
Only one thought, one goal

Rescue the life of the child
But the morrow came
And frightened, she saw
The child was dead
And no longer needs any bread.

Yehudit Tsernatski, of blessed memory

[Page 124]

My Kaddish

I had a son
Talented, good, fine
I had my kaddish – he would be
Brought up to be a proud and good Jew
I would always hope, strive
To be at his bar mitzvah

Who will now say kaddish for me
Who will now cry and lament for me?

Justice

Justice

Come, stand up and demand
For the spilled blood of the millions
Where the murderers stretched out their hands
The Jewish blood was spilled
Justice!
Do not permit the murderers to wipe away their sins
Hand out a punishment
For the murders
Justice
Come, stand up and demand
For the spilled blood of the six million

Revenge

May their green fields be cursed
May their beautiful pure forests be cursed
May the rays of the sun no longer shine upon them
May the rain and dew no longer dampen them
You, dear beloved God,
Send a hellish horrible fire upon them

[Page 125]

Grant the Jewish mother her one and only revenge
Prepare for her children's murderers a horrible revenge
Only one consolation in our life
You can now give us
That we should live
To see and to hear
How the murderous people and lands
Will be wiped out of the world
Because all that is holy is dead
They trod upon all with their feet
Tens of thousands little children
Burned, destroyed.

Last letters

Translated by Sara Mages

Letters from Shlomo and Yitzchak Rabinovitz to their sisters in Israel.
(They were concealed in a bottle, which was hidden by a gentile in Svir, and later transferred to Israel).

Svir, 10 Nisan 5702 [28 March 1942]

To my beloved sisters!

"O Lord God to whom vengeance belongs; O God to whom vengeance belongs, shine forth". [The Book of Psalms 94:1]

I'm hiding at this place all that's left. Outside the sword will bring death. Very soon the Lithuanians will enter the town. There is no other way, but to try to escape. To where? The roads are very dangerous. A torrent of blood and tears, entire groups are being led like lambs to the slaughter.

Master of the universe!
Are you putting an end to all the survivors?

I justify my sentence! I didn't immigrate to Eretz-Yisrael despite all the obstacles.

[Page 126]

We have sinned because we didn't build the Land of Israel. It is difficult to describe what we have gone through and what is awaiting us, the poets and writers will handle it.

Love the homeland, the Holy Land.
Build it, so future generations will not know massacres, pogroms, exile, etc.

Shalom to you,
Maybe forever
Remember Shlomo. It is a right to die in Eretz-Yisrael, but I apparently did not earn it.

* * *

Translated by Mindle Crystel Gross

Chanele, Feygele,

Dear children, it is probable that we are writing to you for the last time. It has not yet been said aloud, but regrettably it will be so, and I say goodbye to you. Be well, and take pleasure in your families, each of you. Chanele, Feygele, I write and my hand trembles and I say goodbye to you. Be well.

Your brother, Yitzhak

* * *

I forgot the most important thing.

I'm hiding in this place all that's left, I shouldn't specify. We hid all of our belongings with Metzik Paleika.

[Page 127]

The Demise of Svir

by Dr. Chanoch Swironi

Translated by Mindle Crystel Gross

Edited by Toby Bird z"l

It was a Shabos afternoon - in 1941. Four days earlier, Hitler had declared war against the Soviet Union. All the telegraph agents reported details about Hitler's move into Russia. Here and there one could even find a telegram with the names of cities and towns in Lithuania, and White Russia which were actually in Nazi hands.

The politicos in the newspapers and on the radio kept on saying that the people need to remain calm because the war with Russia is a total error, and Hitler will be broken there in Russia. It was said and written everywhere that the Hitler power will be defeated, that that is where he will be buried.

There were also Jews who, upon receiving these news reports, breathed easier - eventually, we will live to witness Hitler's demise.

Bat-Sheva sat in sadness, wringing her hands, not entering into the conversation with a single word, and soon she broke out into terrible weeping…

Bat-Sheva, what is wrong with you? they asked her.

She answered:

You are all talking about Hitler's end. What good does that do me? Who knows what is happening now in Svir? Who knows whose blood they have already spilled there?

[Page 128]

And Bat-Sheva's heart knew full well. Svir Jews in the whole world had no reason why to breathe easier. Already in the first days, the Nazis had spilled innocent Jewish blood. Actually there began at that time the terrible martyrdom of our nearest and dearest in Svir and surrounding areas.

**Yekhiel and Khaye-Yoel,
of blessed memory, and the family**

That Shabos, June 25th, 1941, the Nazis were already present in Svir. The first victim was Velvl from Mezolitz, who was going to buy something. He was stopped on his way and immediately murdered, and his body thrown into a field of corn. They searched for him for a couple of months. They wanted to give him a proper burial, but they were unsuccessful in finding his body. Only when the peasants cut down the cornstalks, did they then find him, and bring his dead body back to Svir.

A couple of days later, they murdered the teacher Engel in the Alshever Forest. He was Rivke Ayzikov's husband.

In the early weeks, the German gendarmes, together with the Polish police,

[Page 129]

searched for Communists. Just as they had suspected the teacher Engel to have been a Communist, they immediately also arrested two other Svir teachers, the sisters Basye and Freyde Resnik. They, however, were successful in convincing the German officer, that they were not Communists and he freed them. Shmuel Resnik was also tattled upon, that he was a Communist, and he too, was freed.

**Avrum Yitskhak and Rokhl Miller,
of blessed memory, with their sons**

It was worse for Mikhl Donishevski and Leybl Solamyak. Mikhl was Yankev Liber Viner's son-in-law. He was a blacksmith by trade, but he was active with the Soviets. Leybl Solomyak was a Soviet policeman.

[Page 130]

Mikhl was caught in a forest near Svir, but he was a strong youth and delivered a blow to the German policeman and ran away. He then took refuge with Leybl Solomyak near Duberyan. They were discovered there and both were shot.

**Hershl-Nosn Vaynshteyn,
of blessed memory and his family**

After the raid on the Communists, the long siege of forced labor began. For this purpose, the Judenrat was formed, with Chaim Resnik at its head. Its duty was to send the healthy boys and girls to work in the surrounding area.

The Svir Judenrat was composed of decent people who, without doubt, meant well. Among his co-workers were Chanoch Zlatayavke, Yosef -Chaim, Shmuel, Shloyme-Velvl's son-in-law and others, and yet, the Svir Judenrat had a terribly and sad happening during the first months.

The Germans demanded 21 workers for Great Vileyke. The Judenrat, however, did not understand the terrible purpose and sent 21 healthy youths. Chaim Zlatayavski even sent his own son, Yosef.

The end was sad – everyone was locked in a barn, instructed to undress, totally naked and then they burned them alive.

Among the 21 who perished so tragically in Greater Vileyke were Yosef Zlatayovke, Yakov Dobkin, Chaim Shapira, Zalman Zeltser, Hirshe-Leyb Kamin's son, Shmuel-Yosef Potashnik, Aharon Donishevski, Yehoshua Tzakh, Shimon Blyakher, Katriyel

Antsilevitch (Esther-Malke's son), Chana Katz, Yona Svirski (Pesse Yerachmiel's son), Eliyahu Epshteyn and Israel Svirski (Aharon the bathhouse keeper's son).

[Page 131]

**Yisroel-Meir Potashnik,
of blessed memory, and the family**

Several months passed and then a separate ghetto for Jews was established in Svir.

At first, the ghetto was from Keyle Gershovits to the synagogue courtyard and Moshe Miller's house. Pg. 132 We were not permitted on the other side of the street. A little
later on, the ghetto was reduced in size and it was concentrated almost entirely in the synagogue courtyard.

[Page 132]

**Falye (Rafael) and Berta Svirski,
of blessed memory**

The Jews of Svir were required to wear, as were Jews everywhere – yellow patches above their hearts and on their backs.

A couple of hundred men had to go to work early to Dubelyan, Kameroye, Starovyaski and Stratsi. Svir Jews also worked far away from Svir, in Kenye, Verye and Zezner. The Judenrat was responsible for assigning the workers.

No one was paid for work. If the work was not done well, or if the policeman thought that they were lazy, they were beaten.

The workers got little food and were able to get some through the Christian smugglers.

[Page 133]

The work was difficult. Very often the Jews had to go on foot, 15 km each way. Once German gendarmes came from Ashmene and demanded a lot of gold and pieces of jewelry from the Judenrat. Very quickly, the Judenrat complied with everything and they left.

**Shlome–Hershl Ayzikovitz,
of blessed memory**

The ghetto in Svir was not fenced-in – without barbed-wire and without a gate, and was considered to be a *free ghetto* , but it existed only to the end of 1942. At that time, the Svir ghetto was liquidated and everyone was taken to Mikhalishak. There were only left in Svir approximately 160 men, mostly artisans, i.e., tailors, shoemakers, carpenters, etc.

As long as the 60 men remained in Svir, those in Mikhalishak were better off, because they brought them food from Svir. A couple of months later, they too, were chased out of Svir. At the beginning of 1943, there were no longer any Jews in Svir.

[Page 134]

It was terribly crowded in the Mikhalishak ghetto. There were 15 or more people in one small room. The ghetto was fence-in and the entrance and exit could only be through a gate. There were Jews there from the surrounding area, and all suffered terribly.

However, it did not last long. The Mikhalishak ghetto was also liquidated and the Svir Jews from there went in different directions. Some were brought to the Vilna ghetto, but many went to Vevy, Zeznit and Kenye.

One portion of Svir Jews was told that they were supposedly to be sent to the Kovno ghetto, but they were actually brought to Ponar and they were killed there, along with another 6,000 Jews from the surrounding towns.

Ben-Tsiyon Gitlin with Khaye, his wife, of blessed memory

Kenye too, was surrounded on all sides and everyone there was murdered. From Vevye and Zeznir, the younger people were taken to concentration camps and a few of them remained alive.

[Page 135]

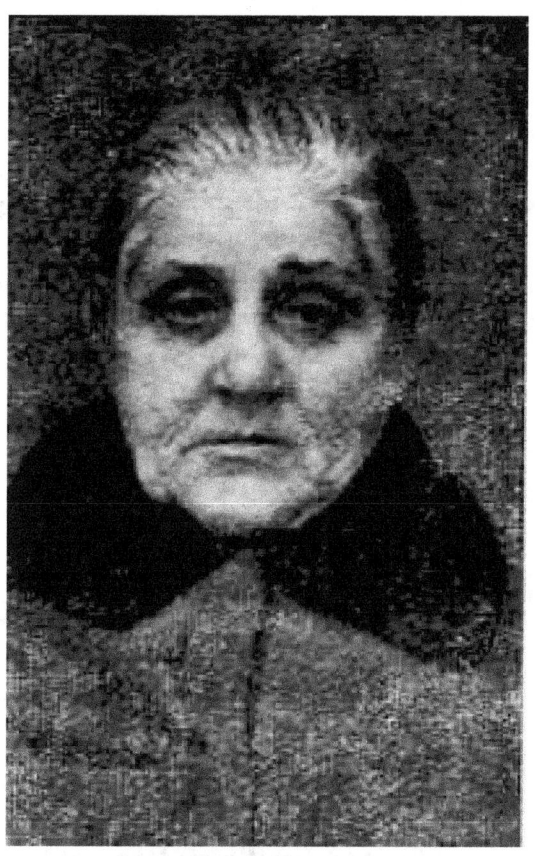

Fayne Papisik, of blessed memory

The same fate was met by the Svir Jews in the Vilna ghetto. Only a few Svir Jews survived because they ran away into the forest and joined the partisan divisions. Among them were: Berl Reznik, Zalman-Mikhl Reznik, Chaim Meltzer, Hirshl Drevyatski and Feygl Tsakh.

Berl Resnik and Chaim Meltser became part of a Russian defense group and Hirshl, Reygl and Zalman joined a Jewish defense division with the name *Nekome* (Revenge)., whom they found near the Naratser River.

When the Germans once attacked the forest, Feygl and Hirshl perished.

[Page 136]

Later on, both sisters, Basye and Freydl, came to Zalman. They had succeeded in escaping from the Vilna ghetto while on their way to work. Pg. 136 Along the way, they tore off the yellow patches and disguised themselves as Christians. They walked 120 km until they finally dragged themselves to the Naratse River, and there they found their brother Zalman.

When they liquidated the Vilna ghetto, a small portion of the Svir Jews was sent to Estonia. There, a short time afterwards, they were murdered.

The ashes and bones of the Svir martyrs are found in Vilna, Ponar, Kenye, Vevye, Zezir and Estonia and in the camps of Germany.

This in short, is the history of the demise of and annihilation of the Jews of Svir.

The greater portion of the Svir martyrs perished around Passover in 1945.

Just when it was spring, when everything grows and blooms, was the innocent blood of hundreds of Svir men, women and children spilled, just as Bialik had pictured earlier in his poem:

> The sun was shining,
> The acacia was blooming.
> And the slaughterer slaughtered.

[Page 137]

Memories of an Eyewitness

by Tsivye Dobkin

Translated by Mindle Crystel Gross

Edited by Toby Bird z"l

The sudden eruption of the war in Europe in September, 1939 hit hard and shattered the Jewish population of Svir. A portion was mobilized into the Polish military. The police and higher officials immediately left town. For a short time, Svir was left with no power. The Christians remained quiet, maybe because a rumor circulated about the Ribbentrop-Molotov agreement, that Svir would become part of the Soviet section. A deathly quiet permeated the town. The stores were closed. The windows of the houses were boarded up, and Jews waited nervously for the next day. Nevertheless, they quietly organized, and the firefighters took over control, arranging a watch each night for the residents.

With the entrance of the Soviets (Red Army), the town breathed more freely. The first to announce the news was Yosef Motkin. He ran with joy through town, shouting for the windows to be opened: the sun is rising in the east.

Their autos remained standing in place and on a microphone they kept making speeches to the public. Right away, a second power was nominated, at whose head was Kuzma. The Jews were represented by Yankl Milner and Yoylke Motkin (all former Communists). A couple of months later, Yoylke, who was beloved in all circles, died suddenly. His death left a strong impression. At his huge funeral, the military brass band played along with the band of the firefighters. Speaking from Zelig Svirski's balcony, Shmuel Reznik

[Page 138]

eulogized him. Upon his grave were laid garlands of flowers from all the organizations, institutions and towns.

The Jewish economic life in time improved. Jewish shopkeepers sold out their merchandise and were able to exist from this. A large portion of the youth worked as officials in various state posts. Artisans and draymen organized. Sadakin and Meir Svirski opened state stores of manufacture and fancy goods production. Chanoch Zlatavyanke opened a stall for books and toys. Movies were played three times a week. Frequent shows were presented for the youth. Many new houses were built on the other side of the bridge and gave the town a new appearance. Shlomo Rabinovitch was the teacher in the Jewish elementary school, which had only three classes. The older generation continued to pray in the synagogue, and lived their lives in their previous traditional manner.

And this is how we lived until June 22, 1941, when Hitler attacked the Soviet Union. On June 23rd, they were already in Svir. The first Germans came on motorcycles and caused fear in everyone. Brash was the head of the civilian power, and they installed police from the local Polish population, and not waiting long, began to work on the Jews who immediately recognized the fate which awaited them. Laws began to be published, such as wearing a yellow patch, not walking on the sidewalk, and sweeping the streets, most especially on Sundays when the Polish population went to church. The first blow was the arrival of the news that the 21 men, who had been sent for work in Vileyke through the recently created Judenrat, had all been burned. (It hit our own family especially hard because we suffered three victims: my brother, Yankl, my cousin, Yosl and a relative, Kasriyel Antsilevitch.

[Page 139]

They broke everything. They turned the synagogue into a grain storage facility, and the Torahs and religious books were burned in the street, in front of everyone's eyes.

Many refugees arrived in town from the surrounding little villages, such as Farbradz, Nementchin, Sventsiyen, and so forth.

When the ghetto was established, Chanoch and Khaye, Margute, Shaykin and a family of five were living in our house.

When the Svir ghetto was liquidated, everyone was transferred to Mkhalishak. I was working in Duberlan at various field jobs along with my sister Tcherne, Sore the rabbi's daughter, Zelde Mikhnovitch and Mashke Svirski. Once a week, we were permitted to take products by wagon to Mikhalishak ghetto, alone and with no one's help. We used to travel through little side roads until we arrived there, and the joy was great from our family. We were saving them from hunger which was rampant in the ghetto.

Meanwhile, the defense was organized. In this arena, their first job was to set fire to the Balkover courtyard where my sister Blumke worked. They killed four policemen in the neighboring villages who collaborated with the Germans. After completing the work season, we were assembled from all the villages and taken to the Mikhalishak ghetto. We were there only two weeks. It was terribly crowded. About 20 people lived in one house under difficult circumstances. The Christians would arrive at the fence with their products and exchange food for the few items we still owned from Svir. And this is how our troubled life went. The elderly and weak Jews died out.

[Page 140]

A short while prior to the liquidation, a portion of the youth was taken out of Mikhalishak to Vilna. Among them was also our Blumke. On the eve of the liquidation from the Mikhalishak ghetto, we were informed that whoever had ties with family in Vilna had the right to go there. Our family then relocated to Vilna.

We were quartered on Hospital Street with another family in one room. Vilna had already gone through a couple of liquidation actions, but many Jews still remained. I was working in a grain storage facility in town at that time. There too, in the work-place, we exchanged with the Christians for various products and secretly brought them into the ghetto.

The terrible news about the slaughter at Ponar reached us quickly when the bloody clothing of the 500 victims was brought into the ghetto the next day. Among them, the greatest portion was Svir Jews.

At the same time, we found out that the transport of young women who were taken to Lithuania, among them Khanke the rabbi's daughter, had also been murdered. The rabbi eulogized them in the Vilna synagogue. A short while later, all the Vilna refugees, including my two sisters and me (older people, among them, my father and mother, were meanwhile left) and we were taken to Estonia.

Women were kept separate there. The surrounding population helped us a lot. Nine months later, we were transferred to a second camp. The guards were Estonian. The leader was an S.S. man. Conditions were much worse there. We lived in barracks

[Page 141]

and worked at digging canals – hard physical labor.

Later on, they brought Svir Jews to this same camp; Rabbi Eliyohu Zlatavyanke, Shmuel Reznik and others. During a selection, when they led a group of people to their death, I witnessed a horrible picture. I saw how they dragged Eli Zlatavyanke, barefoot, on a sled in a terrible frost because he could no longer walk by himself. There, I once accidentally also saw my father. I only recognized him by his eyes. He was entirely covered with gray hair, bent, barely dragging himself. I ran quickly with joy to tell my sisters, and when I turned around, I lost sight of him. I never saw my father again.

After being in Estonia for a year, in 1944, my sisters and I were transferred to Germany to the infamous camp of Shtuthof. The trip took three days by boat. The conditions were unbearable. They jammed many people in like animals into a large room, so tightly packed, that it was not even possible to stand, and in case someone lost his place, he could no longer push his way back.

We only ate twice a day, enough to sustain life. At lunch-time, they distributed food from a trough like for animals, cold soup with a couple of rotten or frozen potatoes. Quite often, we would also find worms. There was one bowl for two people, no spoons. In the evening, we got potatoes and bread. There was roll-call twice a day. The selections took place while we stood at roll-call. They led to one side the elderly and weak, and many times, divided families. Dramatic scenes took place at this separation. In spite of all the pain, the will to live was strong

[Page 142]

in everyone, and after every selection, we breathed easier and knew that our lives would continue for a certain time, and maybe we would even be able to await the wonderful hour of liberation.

The guards were very strict. The camp was encircled with a high electronically-charged fence, and from high towers, large searchlights lit up the surrounding area. After being in Shtuthof for six months, a group of women, to which my sisters, Blumke Dinenshteyn and I belonged, was sent to do farm work for a German. There we met Russian female prisoners, and many German workers. This was at the end of 1944. There we found out from a German Communist woman, that the Nazi army was suffering terribly and their end was imminent. We received this kind of news with joy, but we worried whether we would live to see this. We also found out the reason why we had been transferred from Estonia – it appeared that the Germans had simply retreated from there.

There was no guard where we were working, and we felt free. However, we did not remain there long. Again we completed our work, and brought back to the same hell in Shtuthof. A large percentage of our acquaintances were no longer living. The rest all looked like skeletons, living shadows. There we met Feyge the rabbi's daughter, Sonye Khadash, Khaye Spektor, Paulie Svirski. As we subsequently found out from a woman from Mikhalishak, in her section in Shtuthof, there were still many from Svir, such as Esther-Malke Blakher, Khane and Lete Konagovitch, Frumke and Batya'ke Miller, as well as Yehude-Velvl's two girls. At the beginning of 1945, with the Red Army approaching

[Page 143]

closer to the border of Germany, they herded us on foot deeper into central Germany. All the highways were clogged with German military, and we were led through side roads. This was in January, snow, and at night we slept frozen, hungry, in a stable. We received no food, and the next day, again through the snow. We dragged ourselves like this for a couple of weeks, until they finally put us up m a large stable in a village. There was no water, so we drank only snow. Our food consisted of a couple of potatoes with the peels. The hygiene and sanitation conditions were terrible, impossible to describe it. We lay in a swamp and from the cold the majority of people had frozen feet. The insects crawled on us and virtually devoured us. Many epidemics broke out – dysentery and typhus, and death cut down hundreds of victims every day. I witnessed before my very eyes, the death of Tillie Svirski and both of my sisters – Tcherne and Blumke. The first occurred three days before the liberation and the second three days after the liberation. Imagine my situation, coming to the sorrowful conclusion that I am the youngest of our many-branched family. My brother Yankl was among the first to be murdered. My parents were certainly no longer alive. We had managed to stay together the entire time, suffered through difficulties, many times looked death in the eyes, and here, on the threshold of being free, cruel death separated us forever.

For six weeks we lay in the stable, until the Russians liberated us. One night earlier, we had heard shooting. We lay in fear the entire time, that we would actually be murdered here at the very last minute when they would have to surrender, as had actually occurred in many camps.

[Page 144]

Later, cases were described how people were transported from camps, were thrown alive into the sea. In the early morning, however, the girls came from the kitchen, those who worked in the village, and told
us the news that there were no guards and we were free. Everybody was in a weakened condition and could not move, but with their last ounce of strength, fell upon one another, kissing, with tears in their eyes, and

at that moment, I saw my old home and the thought nagged in my brain: am I the only one left of the family? Will I yet meet those whom I love somewhere, where?

For six weeks, we were in the stable, and of the 1500 people who were taken there, only 400 remained alive at the liberation, among them, sick and invalids, many of whom later died.

On that same day, the Soviet military passed through, and the officers paid us a visit. They went over to each of us individually and clasped our hands with good-natured smiles on their faces, which reawakened in us the belief and trust in people, which over the course of years had died. In accordance with their orders, they took us on wagons to a neighboring village. Feygele and I, being unable to stand on our feet, were carried to the wagons. A week later, a hospital was opened in the village. The doctors were Russian, and the head nurse was Jewish, and the rest of the technical; work was done by Germans. We were treated well in the hospital. I recovered my strength quickly and grew healthy. Many underwent various operations, others suffered amputations of fingers and a couple, of their legs. After leaving the hospital, we were free and could gravel wherever we wanted.

[Page 145]

Khaye Spektor and I, who had left the hospital at the same time, in March, 1945, decided to go home. We were pulled towards returning there, to the place of our birth, and maybe we could find someone from our families.

We arrived in Svir during the summer when all of the surrounding nature is so beautiful and in bloom. But our hearts were quite frozen, cold. It was on a sunny Sunday and some Christians whom we saw, exhibited a strange wonderment at our arrival, that some Jews of Svir had remained alive. Others reacted in the opposite manner, resulting in tears at our meeting. The town was destroyed and wiped out. The entire main street was either half or totally burned out. From the synagogue courtyard – other than the synagogue – there was nothing left. Our house had been burned. I was at Gutl Yoel's who lived at Zalman -Mikhl Fisher's house, who received me warmly.

With our arrival, the total of rescued Jews rose to 11, and by the time we left the town, the total had risen to 40.

We could not remain in Svir for any length of time. There were too many memories everywhere of our former life.

Today, only a pile of ashes remains.

The loneliness and strangeness around us freed us to continue to wander and look for a secure corner, and the only end-point for me was Eretz Yisroel, to meet with my sister and brother.

After spending two months in Svir, almost all the Svir Jews left. After spending a short time in Lodz, we left for Germany.

At the end of 1946, I left Germany and traveled on the ship Latrun to Cyprus, and finally, seven months later, arrived in Eretz Israel, a short time before the birth of the State of Israel.

[Page 146]

A Svir Partisan

by Chanoch Drutz

Translated by Mindle Crystel Gross

Edited by Toby Bird z"l

While in the Vilna ghetto, several youths from Svir decided that something had to be done, and not to sit and wait for death. They sought an opportunity to run away and join the partisans. They were Berl Reznik, Chaim Meltzer, Hirshl Drevnitski, Fayvl Tsakh and Zalman Reznik. Three of them perished, two remained alive.

One of the Svir partisans later became well-known in the entire area, and even received two medals from the Soviet military power. This was Berl Reznik, Kaufman's son.

The decision to join the partisans was made by Berl after he found out that his brother Ruven-Meir and his entire family had been shot in Ponar, and his brother Yitskhak and his family had been murdered in Kenye. Heroic Berl could not rest, remain passive. He worked out plans for a method to run away. He was busy with this day and night, with only one thought – how to get out of the ghetto.

He spoke to several others, sought ties to the underground organization, and at the end, he succeeded in convincing Chaim Meltzer and three other friends, and all five decided to flee.

They bought a revolver and 150 bullets for 25,000 zlotys. They obtained a pass which would allow them to go to work to Lavadisbak and they exited the ghetto.

Saying goodbye to their parents, sisters and brothers was very difficult. The ghetto residents were all of the opinion that these five were heading towards a sure death.

[Page 147]

Hirshl Drevitzki, of blessed memory

Even Shmuel, Berl's older brother, asked him tearfully:

– Where are you going, Berl?

– And Berl replied:

– I will go wherever I can.

They left quite early with all the workers and went together as far as Lavadishak. At that point, they tore off the yellow patches, and walked on foot for about 40 km, until they arrived at the Kotlavker forest in the evening.

There they met a Christian acquaintance and spent the night with him, as well as the next day.

He treated them well, fed them, and in the evening, harnessed his horse and took them to a Christian who lived about 12 km from Svir.

[Page 148]

They stayed several days in the attic of this Christian. They gave him money and he bought them a gun.

They left and went to another place, where Chaim Meltzer's sister, Reiche Keile, was hiding. . Chaim remained there one month, then he joined a Lithuanian partisans group and fell in one of their actions.

Chaim Meltzer, of blessed memory

Berl and his friends decided to go on, and on their way they met a Jewish partisan, who was on his way to Lintep to blow up railroad tracks. He told them, that if they give their commander the gun, he will allow them to join their group, as partisans.

They thought that they had no choice, so they gave up the revolver. They followed the man about 30 kilometers and finally he asked them to wait.

[Page 149]

Feivel Tzach, of blessed memory

And he went, assumedly to ask the commander. They never saw him again.

So they walked on, and later they met a Christian, who showed them the way to Jews who were living in a forest.

Three weeks later, they met a partisan who knew the other youths, and thanks to him, they arrived in a Russian partisan division.

This division consisted of 200 men, among whom were 17 Jews. They camped in the forest 20 km from Miyadl.

The entire partisan brigade was composed of 12 divisions, and the leader of all was Markov, a Polish teacher from Sventsiyon, whom the Poles had once incarcerated in prison for Communist activities. Markov received his directives from the military

[Page 150]

power in Moscow.

At the beginning, the partisans lived in dug-out trenches in the forest. Later, they spread out across the fields and roads in order to carry out various responsibilities.

The group which Berl Reznik joined was responsible for blowing up bridges, causing trains to leave the tracks, cutting down telephone poles, and finding out the German locations, destroying the German camps, fomenting agitation among the population against the German fascists, and defending the poor peasants from German attacks.

The entire brigade consisted of almost 2500 people and was considered to a sort of second Russian army which was at the back of the Germans.

The brigade had its own radio station, and at the end of 1943, everybody had ammunition, a rifle or an automatic.

By 1944, they controlled the area very well, and they even took up official residence in the villages where no German dared to enter.

Berl was with a group in a village 10 km from Sametove. He and five Christians were given the responsibility of burning the Stratser Bridge. They remained in the forest during the day, and at night they went to their appointed place.

They went to several peasants and ordered them to harness their horses. They loaded the wagons with straw and wood, and of course, kerosene, and in the dark of the night, they arrived at the bridge.

They ignited the straw and wood beneath the bridge, and when the Germans came, the bridge was already burned.

[Page 151]

Eliezer Gabay, of blessed memory

This was Berl Reznik's first assignment. A couple of weeks later, he went to cut down telephone poles near Semetove.

He also participated in chasing away the German garrison near Myadl. He was in the group that burned Semetove and chased from there the German military. From then on, Semetove was actually in partisan hands.

Berl exploded a train-line near Smargan and blew up train-lines in other places.

He received two awards for his bravery and whenever partisans are thanked publicly, the name of Berl Reznik is mentioned.

One time, when he had to go through some deep water, he fell into a hole and began to drown. Luckily, another partisan dragged him out.

[Page 152]

Berl used his good name with the partisans in order to help the Jews in the forests and in the dug-out trenches. He once found in one of these dug-out trenches Aharon Shapire with his wife and son, Ayzik Yaffe and Rayze, Zalman Renik and his two sisters, Khasye and Greyde, Yitskhak Meltzer and Yitskhak Fisher and their families.

From that time on, he did not rest, searching for Svir forest people. He received permission from the commander and brought them a sack of potatoes, flour, meat and clothing, and he also gave them a horse so that they could bring trees and be able to build a better hiding place.

The commander was so pleased with Berl that he once went with him to the hiding-place to meet his acquaintances. When Belrl would arrive to see the Svir Jews, it was a true holiday for them, because they knew that he was saving their lives.

And so weeks and months flew by until the Soviet regular army took control of the Svir area.

Berl Reznik ran 12 km on foot in order to notify the Svir Jews that they were free.

And that is how a Jewish youth from Svir had a part in the large victory over the Hitleristic bands, and all from Svir everywhere are proud of him.

[Page 153]

Christian – Angels

by Dr. Chanoch Swironi

Translated by Mindle Crystel Gross

Edited by Toby Bird z"l

1.

At a time when six million Jews were in such a gruesome and wild manner eradicated by human-animals, burned and silenced, at a moment when every Jew remembers his nearest who, at the hands of barbarians, died so tragically, he grits his teeth in pain, and there awakens in him a feeling of revenge, and upon his lips there arises a black curse, at that very moment, his breath will virtually catch, and he will not believe, and he will imagine that this is a dream, when he will hear what the rescued Svir Jews relate. And a true picture will open up before his eyes. He will suddenly discover that there, in our faraway home, there live not only human-animals, not only wild sadists, but also people-angels, saints, before whom every Jew and every person must bow his heads and kneel before them as before a holy figure. Whoever listens to these stories of the rescued Svir Jews becomes aware that there in the forests and in the villages surrounding Svir, live such Christians about whom children and grandchildren will have to tell legends, and writers will have to portray them as the thirty-six secret saints, and there will not be enough words to praise and to thank them.

Among these people-angels, Christian saints, who deserve to be part of the history of the Jewish martyrdom such as khasidim of the nations of the world, we must mention, with a

[Page 154]

feeling of honor and thankfulness seven Christian families: 1) Stanislav and Vzane Mikhnavits of Stupenat; 2) Stanislav Valeyke of Lushtsike; 3) The Kot family of Staravyatke near Konstantinove; 4) Mikadam

Tsernyavski near Zalyadz; 5) Andrej Salkovski near Varnyan; 6) Ossip Telika near Zyanovyets and 7) Kurkus near Stratsi.

2.

At the very beginning, when the Germans entered, an unknown Christian saved a Jew from certain death. This also happened with Moshe Svirski, Alikim the Black's son. He intended to sneak out of Svir and flee to a Christian whom he knew who lived in a small village about three km from town. However, on his way, he was captured and the German officer instructed two Polish policemen to shoot him in a nearby forest.

The two Christian young men loaded their rifles and led him to a little hill. Along the way, Moshe heard the two policemen speaking to each other, saying that they had pity for him, and he should not be shot. When they entered the forest, one of the Christians told him not to be afraid because they would only shoot into the air, but he must fall down immediately and lie there until nightfall, and when it will be very dark, he could run away from there.

And so it was. Moshe ran away at night, not to Svir, but to Selevits, a village five km from town. Everybody in Svir was certain that he had been shot.

Several months passed.

Yom Kippur, 1941. Moshe accidentally had the opportunity to work on the road not far from Selevits. As he worked, he noticed a peasant carrying a little stick and looking at him oddly, as if he knew him, and suddenly, when he came closer, Moshe, frightened,

[Page 155]

saw how the peasant dropped his stick and began to cross himself, calling out: *Oh, Jesus,* running over to Moshe quickly, grabbing him, kissing him and shouting:

– Thank God you are alive. Everyone said that they had shot you on the little hill in the forest.

Vzane Mikhnovits from Stupenat

It seems that this Christian knew Moshe very well, and this was **Stanislav Mikhnovits** from Stupenat. Those Svir Jews whom he rescued call him Uncle Stas to this very day.

Moshe told Stas how he had been rescued, and Stas told him that he himself would have done the same thing. Incidentally, he told him that if he found himself in danger, he could always come to him to Stupenat and hide there.

[Page 156]

Stas left and Moshe continued to work. His situation however, became more difficult from day-to-day, and Moshe went to Stupenat.

At that time, Stas happened to have a number of guests, and they advised him to wait in the kitchen. When the guests left, Vane, Stas' wife, prepared the table and made a holiday supper. The entire family sat around the table. They had eight children, five sons and three daughters. They were all very friendly to Moshe, although they knew quite well that if a Jew was found with them, they would all be killed.

When the children went to bed, Stas remained sitting with Moshe until three a.m. and worked out a plan – how to save him.

Moshe left and Stas in the meantime, prepared a secret corner in the attic of the stable, a small room surrounded by wood and straw.

During the night of March 28th, 1942, Moshe arrived and immediately climbed into his place in the stable attic.

3.

He lay there almost seven months, all alone. Stas, Vzane and all the children would bring him food every day, water for washing and even saw to it that he always had something to read.

Meanwhile, Stas was able to receive news about the situation in Svir. The Germans were going to liquidate the Svir ghetto. Moshe asked Stas to rescue his sister Pessl and her family, and Stas agreed. However, along with Pessl and her son, there came Berele Svirski and his elderly mother, a woman of about 65, and his bride, a young girl from Myadl.

[Page 157]

There were now six people living in the attic room, and the question of food arose. As long as Moshe was the only one, Stas managed, but to feed six people was difficult for him.

Stanislav Mikhnavits of Stupenat

Moshe gave Stas the address of a Christian acquaintance of his in Lushtsike, a village two km from Svir, **Stanislav Valeyke**, and told him to explain everything about how they were hiding, and to figure out with him how to get food for them.

To their great joy, Valeyke agreed to bring them food every other Sunday.

Now Stas also brought Moshe Drevyatski, Pesye's husband, and now there were seven people in the stable attic.

For the entire summer, Valeyke supplied them not only with food, but also with various news reports about Svir Jews. Around Rosh Hashana, they found out that Gitl and

[Page 158]

Zalman-Borukh were in the Vilna ghetto, and Valeyke said that he wanted to rescue them as well.

A couple of days later, Gitl and Zalman-Borukh were also in the attic, and even Tsirl's girl, Khaye-Tsipe.

Ten people in a small room in which one could barely turn around. It was tight, but everybody was happy that they found themselves there and not in the ghettos, and that they still had hope at remaining alive.

And so passed days, weeks, months. Once every two weeks, and always on Sunday, Valeyke would arrive from Lushtsike, and bring them food.

Valeyke was to them as a window to the world. He was their newspaper, their radio, and it would be a holiday for the ten Svir people when he arrived. Stas came in every morning to bring them breakfast and to wake them. *Good morning.* Slowly, they became accustomed to his morning visit, so if he was occasionally late, they would be afraid. Who knew what might have happened.

And when he finally did show up, with a cigarette in his mouth and say *Good morning*, they felt relief.

4.

Finally, it became known in Stupenat that Stas had something to do with Jews. They had heard that his opinion about the Jews was not a bad one, that he was speaking of them with a feeling of pity, and this talk also reached the ears of the chief of Stupenat. One winter afternoon, in 1943, he paid a visit to Stas. He told him clearly and precisely that the village residents were speaking badly of him, that he is involved with Jews, and he warned him that if this turned out to be true, he, along with the children, would be shot

[Page 159]

in his own yard, and their bodies would be given as food to the dogs.

Difficult, very difficult to imagine what took place in Stas' house that afternoon. The children and his wife cried and wailed. On one hand, they did not want to cause their father such pain and drive the Jews out to a certain death, and on the other hand, their own lives were also dear.

The ten Svir Jews talked it over and informed Stas that they would leave and free him. They did not want him to perish because of them. Now, to their great amazement, he told them that he would absolutely not let them go to a certain death. He wanted to look for another place for them first.

Four months passed after the Saltis's visit, and he had found no other place. Vzanye and the children were constantly in a state of fear, wailing and complaining, but not one of them wanted to force the Jews out.

That week, something happened. Not far from Stupenat, there was another family from Svir, Yosl Karasin, his wife and child.

Yosl's wife was shot and he and the child fled.

This convinced Stas to decide that another place had to be found for the Jews.

Berele Svirski, his bride and mother went to another peasant in the village of Kiselay, and the other seven Jews, Stas decided to take at night to the village of Kisaley, 12 km away from Stupenat.

Everybody decided to leave and not to put Stas in danger, but Motele Drevyatski had

[Page 160]

a bad leg and could not walk. Stas did not have to give this much thought, harnessed his horse and wagon and drove him.

After walking about two km, Moshe Drevyatski, Pessl and Gitl had to stop. They too, were in very weakened conditions and could not go further. Stas put them in the wagon as well, and was now transporting four Jews in the dark.

They begged him to go back home and to not put his life in danger, but he said:

– Whatever will happen to you will happen to me as well. I will return home only after you will be in a safe place.

After riding one km, they saw three people on a small hill. They stopped and consulted where they should stay, but they noticed the three running away at top speed. They later found out that these three had been Zushke from Mihalishak and his children.

Little by little, through the deep darkness of the night, they arrived close to the Stratsi courtyard. It was about midnight when they had to cross the train-tracks which led to Vilna.

In a house 200 meters from the road, a light shone. They already knew that there were Germans in Stratsi. Music could be heard coming from that house. Soldiers could clearly be seen through the windows, dancing with young women and singing. Stas understood that this is only a party and he consoled the Jews and told them not to be afraid.

But yet, there was a terrible moment when suddenly, two men emerged from the house. But they were singing something and were noticeably drunk.

Meanwhile, the wagon with its passengers continued on.

[Page 161]

An hour later, they arrived at a river. The water-level was high, and there was no discussion whether to cross on foot or to drive the wagon through. Stas knew this place and said that it was quite deep and that they would have to row across. To their good fortune, they found a boat and one by one, rowed across. Stas, his horse and wagon could not go any further. He bid them goodbye, kissed everyone and wished for them that God should save them all, and he hoped that he would be lucky enough to see everyone again – alive.

The seven people remained standing alone on the other side of the river and listened to the wagon as it went further and further away, and when they could no longer hear the footsteps of the horse and the noise of the wheels, they began to walk slowly, step-by-step. They had to carry Motele. Gitl Moshe and Pessl were weak, and yet, they walked. In early morning, finally, they made it to their new place at the Christian Kurkus, who had promised Stas that he would take them in.

In Kurkus' stable-attic, they found Yitskhok Troytsen and his entire family. Also, since the house was situated far from a village and a road, it was safer than in Stupenat. The Svir Jews received food there as well from Velayke.

This young Christian from the Lushtsike forests was then approximately 30 years old, and through various ways, understood how to provide food for all these hidden Jews. He held a certain belief to rescue the Jews, and at every opportunity, he stressed this and said that he sees no nicer or better goal in his entire life.

And so passed several more months.

At the end of July, 1944, the Soviets entered the Svir neighborhood, and those in Svir, Jews along with dozens of others, were freed.

[Page 162]

In Stupenat, Stas arranged a dance to which came Bronislav Valeyke from Lushtsike, all the Svir Jews who had stayed with him in the attic. They danced and sang together with the children of Stas. He, Stas, was overjoyed, like the father of the bride or groom, virtually crying from happiness. The celebration lasted until dawn.

Everyone said goodbye and promised devotion to each other for their entire lives.

When the Svir Jews later arrived in Germany, they sent to Stupenat various packages, and to this very day, they exchange letters as true family. Moshe Svirski now lives in a village not far from Giv'at Brener, and when you visit him, you will find two large pictures on the bed which are the pictures of Stanislav and Vzyane Mikhnovits from Stupenat.

And Moshe Svirski shows these two photos with great pride and says:

– This is Uncle Stas and this is Aunt Vzane.

5.

Fortunately for the Jews of Svir, Stas was not the only Christian who rescued Jews.

Yosl Karasin and Pere Tsakh and Aaron Shapira have similar stories to tell about good Christians.

When the Germans entered Svir on June 24th, 1941, Yosl was living in Dombravke, not far from Svir.

For six months, the Germans did nothing, but at the end of 1941, Karasin's family was also chased into the Svir ghetto. In April, they were taken to Mikhalishak, but when Yosl found out about those who had perished at Ponar, he decided to flee.

[Page 163]

Since he did not want to risk the life of Simele, a young girl of 1½, he gave her to a Christian, Kot, in Staravyaske, near Konstantinove. The Christian told everyone in the village that his sister's little child was being raised by him, but the neighbors suspected something, that this was only an excuse. They wondered why the mother never came to see her child, and began to think that this is a little Jewish girl. There was a hooligan in town, a known anti-Semite, who once took a stick and wanted to kill the Jewish child. Kot's wife ran out of the house to rescue the child, and out of anger, he hit her with the stick and broke her hand.

6.

An interesting episode was experienced by Borukh Mikhnovayets (Mints), who at the outbreak of WWII, lived with his wife and son in Kriveyn. Four km from town, there lived an outstanding tanner and Borukh learned from him how to work with leather.

In August, 1941, the Nazis entered Kriveyn and searched out all kinds of artisans. Borukh was pointed out. Since they needed a lot of boots, Borukh had a lot of work. They treated him well and fed him decently.

At the end of 1942, the Nazis decided to liquidate the Kriveyn ghetto, and Borukh was the only Jew who was saved and taken to Dolhigov. He worked for them until March, 1943, when the partisans attacked the town.

Borukh made use of this opportunity, and together with his wife and six-year old son, fled. For ten days they wandered around Dolhigov and could not make any contact with the partisans.

[Page 164]

Borukh remembered that in the village of Vilevits there lived an acquaintance of his, a Christian, Yashtsik, and he decided to go to him. Maybe he would save them.

In the darkness of the night, they entered the village. Mrs. Yashtsik opened the door in sheer terror. She fed them and Borukh proposed that her husband should save them in a simple manner. He, his wife and child would lie in a wagon. Yashtsik would pile a lot of straw on top of them. He would sit up high upon the straw and it would not occur to the Germans that Jews were hiding below.

And so it was. Yashtsik agreed to Borukh's request, and drove them through ten terrible km. On the Kriveym Bridge, there were Germans posted. Along the way, they had to cross the train-tracks which led from Maladetsne to Palatsk, and there stood a German garrison.

Finally, they arrived in the Pakuts forest, and there they crawled out of the wagon from under the straw and went into the forest. Yashtsik returned home.

For two days, they went hungry and thirsty, until they encountered hidden Jews in their bunker. They remained there a couple of months until, by accident, Borukh met an acquaintance, a Jewish partisan, and through him came into contact with the partisans.

Borukh's first job for the partisans was to set fire to the stash of ammunition in Roksheyn, together with another partisan and they were successful, and they even stole ten rifles.

Soon the partisans found out that he was a good tanner, so they brought him a lot of hides to make into leather, since they were in need of many shoes and boots. The factory in the forest took on from day-to-day a different appearance, until it became a sort of leather factory where there were 40 people working.

[Page 165]

The partisans valued him greatly as a leather specialist, and he used this situation to help the hidden Jews. Among others, he also met in the forest, Fanye Fisher and Leybl Potashnik and helped them a lot.

After the war, Borukh spent a couple of years in Germany, and from there went to America.

7.

No less moving is the story that Pere Tsakh-Grager has to tell:

In 1941, Pere was in Vurniyon with her husband. Dovid Grager was good friends of the local priest and went to him for advice about what to do. The priest advised him not to go to any ghettos since they had a six-month old son. The priest gave them the address of a Christian with whom they could leave the child and he would be responsible for him. Pere did this, and with her husband fled into a forest, and the little boy was brought up by the Christian woman.

Quite often, the Christian woman brought the child to the forest to show him who his parents were.

Regrettably, the child could not remain with them because it became known. Also Pere and Dovid decided to leave that particular forest, so they took back their nine-month old son and gave him to another Christian, Andrej Salkovski and the little boy remained there for more than three years, i.e., until the arrival of the Soviets.

Pere and Dovid were also hidden for two months at the same Christian's home in the attic of the stable. The little boy used to run around in the courtyard and did not know that his

[Page 166]

parents were there. However, they were able to see him quite well through the cracks in the wall.

Since the Christian was afraid to keep them in the attic, he built a sort of bunker for them in the nearby forest. Quite often, Salkovski would walk there with the child, and she would pass close to this hiding-place so that his parents could see him.

One time, someone came to Salkovski and told him that she had seen a Jew in the forest sitting on a tree and crying. So they had to abandon that hiding-place, meeting up with other Jews in a forest six km from Salkovski. It was then difficult for them to see their child during the day. Only at night would they sometimes take a chance and go to Salkovski to see the little boy while he slept.

When the Soviets entered, Pere took the child back and the child would call her *the young mama,* and Salkovski's wife – *the old mama.*

8.

Aaron Shapira hid in Voltsinits, a courtyard not far from Semetove, and there took care of the cows for the Duke Novirovits. In 1942, he had to flee to a forest because it was impossible to remain there. There had gathered in the forest about 300 Jews from all the surrounding areas. One time, Aaron went to a village to purchase food, taking his two sons with him – Yankev 16 and Zalman 12 and Kasriyel's grandchild, also 12. They got food and carried it back to the forest. However, a Lithuanian policeman noticed them and told them to throw the packages away, and to go with him. He turned them over to the (Pg. 167) Germans. Two Germans took them to a field and instructed them to kneel on their knees. There were shots and all three children were killed. Aaron received two bullets to his head, but remained alive. When the Germans left, badly wounded as he was, he dragged himself to a barn where he spent the night, and later, with difficulty, made it back to the bunker where they bathed his wounds and bandaged them. There were no doctors.

[Page 167]

Chaim, Yankev and Zalman Shapira, of blessed memory

For two months, he lay without medical attention. When his health improved, he left with his wife and five-year old, Hirshele, and went to another forest where they found a good person who gave them food. However, he was afraid to hide them, so they left from there as well, continuing until they reached an acquaintance, a Christian – Ossip Talayke, near Zanaryen, who received them well, fed them, gave them a place to sleep in the barn, and even went to the forest, heated a bath and bathed him himself the way a mother would bathe a child.

[Page 168]

Then his wife came and bathed Aaron's wife and Hirshele. They brought them clean underwear and warm clothes and shoes. From that time forward, they were in the forest during the day and at night, they slept in the barn upon straw, and Talayke would bring them food.

Kasriyel, Leybl and Dvora Potashnik, of blessed memory

They spent six weeks there, until they were noticed, so Telayka built a bunker for them in a forest seven km from there. Many Svir Jews later came there:

> Yitskhok Fisher and his family,
> Yitskhok Meltser and his family,
> Zalman-Mikhl Resnik and both sisters and
> Isaac Yaffe and Reyzn.
> Berl Resnik, who was a partisan, would come to them quite often, bringing food.

All those who were there survived, and after the liberation, returned to Svir.

These are all facts which illustrate a humane attitude towards Jews from many Christians in the neighborhood of Svir.

[Page 169]

At the grave of Aaron Shapiro's perished family

All of this took place at a time when Jews were suffering so much at the hands of the Nazi beasts and so it is our debt to record all of these facts.

May those from Svir who are spread throughout the world know and console themselves about what occurred in Eastern Europe during Hitler's time. There emerged in Svir rays of sun which lit up that area and demonstrated that good people live there and whom we have to laud and thank.

[Page 170]

In the Slaughtered Town

by Chaim Nakhman Bialik

Translated by Mindle Crystel Gross

Edited by Toby Bird z"l

From steel and iron, cold and hard and silent,
Forge for yourself – and come!
Come, go into the slaughtered town, see with your eyes,
Touch with your own hands –
Fences, poles, gates and walls,
Upon stones of the street, on all the wood,
The black dried blood and the limbs
Of my brothers, heads and necks
And you should wander about amidst the destruction,
Past walls, broken, with crooked doors,
Past gaping ovens, half-chimneys
Black stones, half burned bricks.
In the streets you will walk with feathers all over.
You bathe in a river, a wide river
Which was created by human bloody sweat.
You tread on entire piles of torn-apart possessions.
These are entire lives, entire lives,
Broken forever like shards.
You walk, you run, you are twisted
Within the destruction
Brass, silver, furs, silk and such,
Torn, ripped into tiny pieces.

[Page 172]

Svir After Hitler's Downfall

by Chanoch Drutz

Translated by Mindle Crystel Gross

Edited by Toby Bird z"l

The first to arrive in Svir after the entrance of the Red Army were the 11 people, i.e: Moshe Svirski and Gitl, Zalman-Borukh, Moshe Drevyatski and his family and Yitskhok Treyts with his family. They found it to be what Bialik portrayed about Kishinev. On the street were scattered large amounts of furniture, torn items, broken glassware, kitchen items, books and assorted papers. Everything jumbled together created a storm of a terrible destruction. Many houses were either totally or partially burned. Of the tower there remained standing only the bottom floor. Also from Eliyohu-Chaim Grager's house, there remained only half. From Eliyohu-Noakh's house, there remained only the barn, but the neighboring houses were almost not ruined. The houses belonging to Fayve Svirski, Yitskhok Meltser, Ruven-Chaim, Yone Svirski and Chanoch Gelgarn, and most especially the entire street where Moshe Miller, Chanoch Zlatayavke, remained intact, as well as Pariser Street.

In the synagogue courtyard, the rabbi's house and Chaim-Yankev's, Avrom-Yitskhok's, as well as the house of study, remained intact.

[Page 172]

From Pariser Street to Troyts', almost all the houses had been burned. , among them also Chaim-Avrum the baker's house.

The cemetery, however, was not touched by the Christians and not even one headstone was destroyed.

Sore-Gitl's house had been burned. She moved into Zalman-Mikhl Fisher's house. When the Christians became aware that she was alive, they returned everything which, one year earlier, they had taken from her house. Drevyatski, Meltser, Moshe Svirski and Troyts found their houses intact.

It was very sorrowful and sad for the 11 people during their first days in town. Every corner reminded them of the dear and beloved who had perished. Every torn item was a reminder of a house where three years earlier, there had lived good people. Death stared at them before their eyes and the 11 rescued could not find a place for themselves.

Slowly, other rescued Svir Jews began to return. Almost every day, someone would come, and in the early weeks, Svir already had more than 40 Jews.

Within the time-frame of the three impossible years, there was contact only between a few of them. Mostly, they did not know about each other.

Only after the liberation did it become known that from Svir, many people remained alive and among the rescued were several children.

Naturally, every rescued Jew had his own story to tell. Each person lived through something.

In the main, there were stories with miracles about good Christians, but from many, there were horrific stories, details about how their nearest and dearest had perished.

[Page 173]

With regret, Vulik Ayzikovski related how he had to leave Shlomo-Hirshl, his father, to a certain death. They were together with Dovid (Berte Berson's son) in Bukhenwald. From there, they were herded, on foot, to the Sudatenland. They suffered hunger along the entire way, and ate grass. Shlomo-Hirshl became weak and could not continue. He remained sitting to rest. The Germans chased both children further on. They stopped in a village in the evening, and waited there the entire night. A couple of hours later, Shlomo-Hirshl also dragged himself there. The following day, he tried to go with them, but was unable to do so. He knew that he would die along the way. He begged the children to greet his wife, Keyle, and the little daughter, Beyletske, who were in Shtuthof. The children left their father to a certain death, and continued on.

And this is how Shlomo-Hirshl died, of hunger on the way to the Sudatenland. He was the son of Mikhl the watchmaker.

Tsivye Rabkin related how her two sisters, Blume and Tcharne, died before her eyes.

Those who were in the camps told about the heroism of Leyzer Gabay.

Prior to the war, he had been the principal of the Rakshits Hebrew elementary school. In the camp, he took upon himself the dangerous work of supplying ammunition to the partisans. He was in charge of purchasing the ammunition and also transporting it to the forest. When the Germans captured him, he had a revolver in his pocket. They tortured him in front of everyone and demanded he turn in his comrades. He had the courage to remain silent. The Germans tortured him almost to the point of death, but did not extract any secrets.

Three of the Svir partisans: Fayvl Tsakh, Chaim Meltser and Hirshl Drevyatski fell in a

[Page 174]

battle with the animals.

Chaim Meltser fell as a member of a Lithuanian partisan division.

Yosef-Chaim hid with a Christian and it was there that he became very ill. Isaac and Reyze wanted to rescue him, and went to the forest. On the way, they were attacked. They succeeded in escaping and Yosef was murdered.

But with these miracles and acts of bravery, one could not live in Svir. It was very seldom that someone had the heart to remain living among the graves and the ruins, and it is no wonder, that almost all those from Svir who had been rescued, as quickly as possible, left for Eretz Yisroel. A small portion of them went to America.

There remained in Svir only several Jewish families. The Svir Jewish community is almost non-existent.

Destroyed was the small, tucked-away little town where Jews had lived for hundreds of years with a satisfactory cultural and community life. A small community was destroyed where Jews, both in the religious sense and national sense, as well as in the economic, could live out their lives in a good way. Most important is that our parents, because of the destruction, perished in a horrible and barbaric way, as did our brothers and sisters, our dearest and nearest friends and acquaintances, who were not fortunate enough to reach the point of liberation. To all of these victims from Svir is this book dedicated. We will mention them all with the old traditional Jewish Kaddish:

Yisgadal v'yiskadash shmey rabo

All of these we will mention with our generations long historical memorials.

[Page 175]

El Male Rahamim

Oh, that my head were waters, and my eyes a fountain of tears,
that I may weep day and night for the slain of my people!
(Jeremiah 8:23)

Do you feel?

There still swirls about the fear of death
And flutters with a cold black wing
And freezes the roots of the hair on one's head
And here and there, from all the black holes
Are seen eyes, silent eyes, looking.
Looking are the souls of the martyrs,
Silent souls
Who as one here in the corner
Pressed together, frightened – and silent
Trembling like pigeons before the slaughter,
Nestling together to the roof, as one

And look long at you with silent eyes
Which ask only without speech
And complain silently the old complaints –
Why, why and again why?

[Pages 176-187]

Yizkor

Transliterated by Esther Snyder

Edited by Yocheved Klausner

רשימת הקדושים והטהורים, יהודי קהלת סביר,
שנשמדו, נשרפו, נטבעו, נרצחו בידי רוצחים טמאים, גרמנים,
ליטאים, פולנים, בימי מלחמת העולם השניה.

דמותם תלוה את יוצאי סביר באשר הם שם וזכרם
ישאר חרות בלבותיהם לעדי עד ולנצח נצחים.

תהיה נשמתם צרורה בצרור החיים.

ה' ינקום דמם.

A list of martyrs & innocents, Jews from the community of Swir, who were slain, burnt, drowned, murdered by the profane murderers, Germans, Lithuanians, Poles during the period of the Second World War.

Their images will follow the Émigrés of Swir wherever they are and their memories will be engraved in their hearts for eternity.

May their souls be bound up in the bond

of everlasting life! May G-d avenge their

blood.

א	ב	ג	ד	ה	ו	ז	ח	ט	י	כ
Alef	Bet	Gimmel	Dalet	Hey	Vav	Zayin	Chet	Tet	Yod	Kaf
ל	מ	נ	ס	ע	פ	צ	ק	ר	ש	ת
Lamed	Mem	Nun	Samech	Ayin	Peh	Tzadik	Kof	Resh	Shin	Tav

Family Name(s)	First Name(s)	sex	Father's Name	Mother's Name	Spouse	Remarks	Page
א Aleph							
ABEL	Tzippe	F					176
ABEL	Nehama	F					176
ABEL	Feige	F					176
AIZIKOVITZ	Mikhal	M					176
AIZIKOVITZ	Slaveh	M					176
AIZIKOVITZ	Shlomo	M					176
ALPEROVITZ	Esther	F					176
ALPEROVITZ	Etel	F					176
ALPEROVITZ	Lea	F					176
ALPEROVITZ	Chana	F					176
ALPEROVITZ	Unknown	F					176
ALPEROVITZ	Avraham Yitzhak	M					176
ALPEROVITZ	Mendel	M					176
ALPEROVITZ	Etel	F					176
ALPEROVITZ	Rahel	F					176
ALPEROVITZ	Chana	F					176
ALPEROVITZ	Minneh Rahel	F					176
ALPEROVITZ	Bunye	M				and family	176
ALPEROVITZ	Israel Zalman	M					176
ALPEROVITZ	Yakhel	M					176
ALPEROVITZ	Moshe	M					176
ALPEROVITZ	Nianeh	F					176
ALPEROVITZ	Dobbe	F					176
ALPEROVITZ	Libbe Rahel	F					176
ALPEROVITZ	David	M					176
ANTCHELEVITZ	Esther Malka	F					176
ANTCHELEVITZ	Catriel	M					176
ב Bet							
BAROVSKY	Eliyahu	M					176
BUSHKANYETZ	Yaakov	M					176
BLIAKHER	Unknown					From Zasvir'	176
BLIAKHER	Berl	M					177
BLIAKHER	Esther	F					177
BLIAKHER	Dobbe	F					177
BLIAKHER	Aharon David	M					177
BLIAKHER	Diske						177

BLIAKHER	Shimon	M					177
BLIAKHER	Benyamin	M				and family	177
BENSMAN	Avraham	M					177
BENSMAN	Sara Beileh	F					177
BENSMAN	Eliezer	M					177
BENSMAN	Mireh	F					177
BERGER	Nahum	M					177
BERGER	Frida	F					177
BERGER	Hirshe	M					177
BERGER	Tzadok	M					177
BERGER	Israel	M					177
BERGER	David	M					177
BERGER	Barukh	M				and family	177
BROMBERG	Eliyahu Chaim	M					177
BROMBERG	Berteh	F					177
BROMBERG	Moshele	M					177
BROMBERG	Hirshe	M					177
BROMBERG	Reizl	F					177
BROMBERG	Barukh	M					177
BERKMAN	Rabbi Abba	M					177
BERKMAN	Devora	F					177
BERKMAN	Netanel	M					177
BERKMAN	Hedva	F					177
BERKMAN	Sara	F					177

ג Gimmel

GABBAI	Leizer	M				and family	177
GOLDMAN	Yitzhak	M					177
GOLDMAN	Feige Chaia	F					177
GOLDMAN	Sara	F					177
GOLDMAN	Asher	M					177
GOLDMAN	Sara	F				Maiden name SCHPIALER	177
GOLDMAN	Unknown	F		Sara			177
GOLDMAN	Eliyahu	M	Idel				177
GOLDMAN	Ida	F				2 children	177
GOLDMAN	Eltzik	M					177
GOLDMAN	Etel	F				2 children	177
GARGEL	Simeh	F			Pesach		177
GARGEL	Lea	F					177
GARGEL	Yankel	M					177
GARGEL	Kopel	M					177

GARGEL	Benyamin	M					177
GARGEL	Reuven	M					177
GARGEL	Yona	M					177
GURVITZ	Sara Beileh	F					177
GURVITZ	Lusie	F					177
GURVITZ	Itte	F					177
GURVITZ	Chaia Radeh	F					177
GURVITZ	Melekh	M					177
GURVITZ	Bendet	M					177
GURVITZ	Zalman	M					177
GURVITZ	Berte	F					177
GURIS	Yohanan	M					177
GURIS	Sara Rivka	F					177
GURIS	Yudel	M					177
GURIS	Malka	F					178
GURIS	Frumeh	F					178
GURIS	Zlate	F					178
GURIS	Chaia Beileh	F					178
GURIS	Esther	F					178
GURIS	Yosef	M					178
GINSBURG	Eliyahu Moshe	M					178
GINSBURG	Chaia	F					178
GINSBURG	Simha	M					178
GINSBURG	Yaakov	M					178
GINSBURG	Devora	F					178
GINSBURG	Chaim Hirshel	M					178
GINSBURG	Diske	F					178
GINSBURG	Feigele	F					178
GINSBURG	Sheindel	F					178
GINSBURG	Devoraleh	F					178
GITLIN	Meir	M					178
GITLIN	Ben Zion	M					and family	178
GERSCHOVITZ	Keileh	F					178
GERSCHOVITZ	Gnyesye	F					178
GERSCHOVITZ	Rivka	F					178
GERSCHOVITZ	Yehuda	M					178
GERSCHOVITZ	Yokheved	F					178
GLEZER	Avraham	M					178
GLEZER	Slaveh	M					178
GLEZER	Unknown	F	Slave				178
GLEZER	Raskeh	F					178
GLEZER	Esther Lea	F				and family	178

GERSHATER	Chana	F					178
GERSHATER	Chanan	M					178
GRAVITZ	Devora	F					178
GENDEL	Nehama	F					178
GROSSMAN	Sheindl	F					178
GELGAR	Henekh	M					178
GELGAR	Keileh	F				2 children	178
GELGAR	Yitzhak	M					178
GELGAR	Malka Devora	F					178
GELGAR	Ezra	M					178
GELGAR	Nehemia	M					178
GELGAR	Eliyahu	M					178
GRINBERG	Sara Rivka	F					178
GRINBERG	Eliyahu Nahum	M					178
GRINBERG	Unknown	M	Eliyhu Nachum				178
GRINBERG	Chaia	F				and family	178
GRINBERG	Beileh	F				Married. 5 children	178
GRINBERG	Unknown	M			Beile	Married. 5 children	178
ד Dalet							
DOBKIN	Eliyahu Avraham	M					178
DOBKIN	Sara Rachel	F					178
DOBKIN	Blumeh	F					178
DOBKIN	Tzerneh	F					178
DOBKIN	Yaakov	M					178
DANISHEVSKY	Mikhal	F					178
DANISHEVSKY	Nehama Rivka	F					178
DANISHEVSKY	Yaakov	M					178
DIMENTSHTEIN	Avraham	M					178
DIMENTSHTEIN	Sara Beileh	F					178
DIMENTSHTEIN	Shimon	M					178
DIMENTSHTEIN	Menuha Beileh	F					178
DIMENTSHTEIN	Reizele	F					178
DIMENTSHTEIN	Henye	F					179
DIMENTSHTEIN	Eliyahu	M					179
DIMENTSHTEIN	Rahel	F					179
DRUTZ	Velvel Zev	M					179
DRUTZ	Sara	F					179

DREVIATZKI	Moshel	M					179
DREVIATZKI	Malka	F					179
DREVIATZKI	Hirshel	M				and family	179
ה Hey							
HAFSHTEIN	Unknown					and family	179
ו Vav							
WEINER	Abba	M					179
WEINER	Hyeneh	F					179
WEINER	Zeldeh	F					179
WEINER	Velvel	M					179
WEINER	Rivkaleh	F					179
WEINER	Rahel	F					179
WEINER	Shaineh	F					179
WEINER	Leibeh	F				and family	179
WEINER	Abba	M		Rachel			179
WEINER	Chaia Devora	F					179
WEINSTEIN	Hirsheh Natan	M					179
WEINSTEIN	Bryneh	F					179
WEINSTEIN	Reizl	F				and family	179
WEISHKONSKY	Avraham	M					179
WEISHKONSKY	Berteh	F				Maiden name DRUTZ	179
WEISHKONSKY	Velvel	M					179
WILKOMIRSKY	Lea Malka	F					179
WILKOMIRSKY	Israel	M					179
WILKOMIRSKY	Rahel	F					179
ז Zayin							
ZANARATZKY	Nehemia	M					179
ZANARATZKY	Artzik	M					179
ZANARATZKY	David	M				and family	179
ZEIDEL	Barukh	M					179
ZEIDEL	Merl	M					179
ZLATAYOVKA	Henekh	M					179
ZLATAYOVKA	Chaia	F					179
ZLATAYOVKA	Yosef	M					179
ZLATAYOVKA	Layaleh	F					179
ZLATAYOVKA	Iteleh	F					179
ZLATAYOVKA	Malka Tzireh	F					179
ZLATAYOVKA	Eliyahu	M					179
ZLATAYOVKA	Esther	F					179
ZLATAYOVKA	Sonie	F				and family	179

ZELTZER	Yehiel	M					179
ZELTZER	Tzipl	F					179
ZELTZER	Zalman	M					179
ZELTZER	Shmuel	M					179
ח Chet							
HADASH	Isaac	M					179
HADASH	Hirshel	M					179
HADASH	Shmuel	M					179
HADASH	Pesye	F					179
HADASH	Leib	F					179
HADASH	Chaia	F				child	179
HADASH	Shlomo	M			Pesie	Married	179
HADASH	Pesye	F			Shlomo	Married	179
HADASH	Lea	F				and family	179
HADASH	Berl	M					179
HADASH	Barukh	M					179
HADASH	Chana	F					179
HADASH	Avraham	M				3 children	179
HADASH	Sender	M					180
HADASH	Avrahamle	M					180
HADASH	Lea	F					180
CHAIAT	Reuven	M					180
CHAIAT	Yosef	M					180
CHAIAT	Chaia	F					180
CHAIAT	Hirshel	M					180
CHAIAT	Batya	F					180
CHAIAT	Devoraleh	F					180
CHAIAT	Chaialeh	F					180
CHAIAT	Esther	F					180
CHAIAT	Henye Lea	F				and family	180
CHAIAT	Yeshaiahu	M				and family	180
ט Tet							
TABARISKY	Chaim	M					180
TABARISKY	Chana	F					180
TABARISKY	David	M					180
TABARISKY	Dabl	M					180
TABARISKY	Zusieh	M					180
TABARISKY	Reizl	F					180
TABARISKY	Unknown	F		Reizl			180
TABARISKY	Aharon	M					180
TABARISKY	Esther	F				2 children	180

TABARISKY	Sonye	F				and family	180
ל Yud							
YANISKY	Moshe	M				Married	180
YANISKY	Unknown	F			Moshe	Married	180
YANISKY	Shalom	M				and family	180
YANISKY	Layahle	F					180
YANISKY	Gedalyahu	M					180
YANISKY	Lea	F					180
YANKELEVITZ	Rahel Lea	F					180
YANKELEVITZ	Tzvia	F					180
YANKELEVITZ	Dina	F					180
YANKELEVITZ	Keileh	F					180
YANKELEVITZ	Shmuel David	M					180
YOEL	Velvel Zeev	M					180
YOEL	Yehiel	M					180
YOEL	Chaia	F					180
YAFFE	Mirl	F					180
YAFFE	Hodel	F					180
YAFFE	Rivka	F					180
YORAN	Betzalel	M					180
YORAN	Yakhne	F					180
YORAN	Devoraleh	F					180
כ Kaf							
CHATZKELEVITZ	Reuven	M					180
CHATZKELEVITZ	Tzerneh	F					180
CHATZKELEVITZ	Efroim	F				2 children	180
CHARMATZ	Yosef	M					180
CHARMATZ	Batya	F					180
CHARMATZ	Barukh	M				and family	180
CHARMATZ	Shalom	M				and family	180
CHARMATZ	Feige	F				and family	180
CHARMATZ	Chana	F				and family	180
KATZ	Alter	M					180
KATZ	Chaia	F					180
KATZ	Mendel	M					180
KATZ	Yaakov	M					180
KATZ	Shlomo	M					181
KATZ	Malka	F					181
KATZ	Moshe Velvel	M					181
KATZ	Merl	M					181
KATZ	Hanan	M					181
KATZ	Feivel	M					181

KATZ	Sara	F					181
KATZ	Zalman	M					181
KATZ	Hirshel	M					181
KATZ	Freidel	F					181
KATZ	Feige	F					181
KATZ	Rahel	F					181
ל Lamed							
LAVANARSKY	Noah	M					181
LAVANARSKY	Etel	F					181
LAVANARSKY	Gershon	M					181
LAVANARSKY	Chaim Mordekhai	M					181
LAVANARSKY	Sara Mineh	F					181
LAVANARSKY	Moshel	M					181
LEVINE	Yitzhak	M					181
LEVINE	Malka	F					181
LEVINE	Saraleh	F					181
LEVINE	Moshe	M					181
LEVINE	Sasha	M					181
LEVINE	Manye	F					181
מ Mem							
MOLLER	Alter	M					181
MOLLER	Beileh	F					181
MOLLER	Leibeh	M					181
MOLLER	Hodel	F					181
MOLLER	Moshe	M	Israel Zeev				181
MOLLER	Rahel Lea	F					181
MOLLER	Avraham Yitzhak	M					181
MOLLER	Masheh	F					181
MOLLER	Ida	F					181
MOLLER	Zeldeh	F					181
MOLLER	Henekh	M					181
MOLLER	Malka Fisher	F					181
MOLLER	Mikhele	M					181
MOLLER	Simeh Beileh	F					181
MOLLER	Simha	M					181
MOLLER	Yitzhak	M					181
MOLLER	Moshe	M	Eliyahu				181
MOLLER	Chaia Keileh	F					181
MOLLER	Mikhele	M					181

MOLLER	Avraham Yitzhak	M					181
MOLLER	Rahel	F					181
MOLLER	Sarale	F					181
MOLLER	Velvel	M					181
MILLER	Feitel	F					181
MILLER	Zeldeh	F					181
MILLER	Yaakov Lipeh	M					181
MILLER	Sara Itte	F					181
MILLER	Chana	F					181
MILLER	Freidel Libbe	F					181
MILLER	Yehoshua	M					181
MILLER	Temeh	F				2 children	181
MILNER	Batya	F					181
MILNER	Tzippe	F					181
MIKHNOVITZ	Avraham Yitzhak	M					181
MIKHNOVITZ	Rahel	F					181
MIKHNOVITZ	Feige	F					182
MIKHNOVITZ	Hirshel	M					182
MIKHNOVITZ	Sara	F					182
MIKHNOVITZ	Yitzhak	M					182
MIKHNOVITZ	Bryneh	F				and family	182
MIKHNOVITZ	Libbe	F					182
MINDEL	Sara Rivka	F					182
MINDEL	Shlomo	M					182
MINDEL	Alter	M					182
MINDEL	Rivka	F					182
MINDEL	Yosele	M					182
MINDEL	Chaia Feitel	F				2 children	182
MELTZER	Chaim	M					182
ס Samech							
SOLOMIYAK	Buneh Lea	F					182
SOLOMIYAK	Leibeh	F					182
SOLOMIYAK	Ben Zion	M					182
SOLOMIYAK	Yankel	M					182
SOLOMIYAK	Moshe Leizer	M					182
SAKHABENZON	Tzemah	M					182
SAKHABENZON	Zeldeh	F					182
SAKHABENZON	Meir Zelig	M					182
SOSENSKY	Chaim	M					182
SOSENSKY	Henye	F					182
SOSENSKY	Yankel	M				2 children	182

SVIRSKY	Eli Natan	M					182
SVIRSKY	Nehama	F					182
SVIRSKY	Dobbe	F					182
SVIRSKY	Yerahmiel	M					182
SVIRSKY	Meir	M					182
SVIRSKY	Muleh	M	Meir				182
SVIRSKY	Zelig	M					182
SVIRSKY	Gruneh	F					182
SVIRSKY	Shmuel	M					182
SVIRSKY	Devora	F					182
SVIRSKY	Tehiya	F					182
SVIRSKY	Yona	M					182
SVIRSKY	Devora	F					182
SVIRSKY	Feeveh	M					182
SVIRSKY	Taikhel	F					182
SVIRSKY	David	M					182
SVIRSKY	Rivka	F					182
SVIRSKY	Yehoshua	M					182
SVIRSKY	Esther	F					182
SVIRSKY	Yankel	M				and family	182
SVIRSKY	Yona Meir Zelig	M					182
SVIRSKY	Moshe	M				and family	182
SVIRSKY	Masheh	F					182
SVIRSKY	David	M				and family	182
SVIRSKY	Leibeh	F				and family	182
SVIRSKY	Aharon	M					182
SVIRSKY	Nehama	F					182
SVIRSKY	Israel	M					182
SVIRSKY	Yitzhak	M					182
SVIRSKY	Velvel	M				and family	182
SVIRSKY	Shlomo Velvel	M					182
SVIRSKY	Reizl	F					182
SVIRSKY	Tileh	F					182
SVIRSKY	Eliyahu	M				and family	182
SVIRSKY	Moshe	M				and family	183
SVIRSKY	David Yehoshua	M					183
SVIRSKY	Ittel	F					183
SVIRSKY	Nisan	M					183
SVIRSKY	Libbe Daneh	F					183
SVIRSKY	Pesele	F					183
SVIRSKY	Henye	F					183

SVIRSKY	Etel	F					183
SVIRSKY	Yitzhak	M					183
SVIRSKY	Rivka	F					183
SVIRSKY	Berl	M					183
SVIRSKY	Lubeh	F					183
SVIRSKY	Mordekhai	M					183
SVIRSKY	Yaakov	M					183
SVIRSKY	Rephael	M					183
SVIRSKY	Berteh	F					183
SVIRSKY	Pesieh	F					183
SVIRSKY	Rahel	F					183
SVIRSKY	Yona	M					183
SVIRSKY	Shmuel	M	Eli				183
SVIRSKY	Itte	F					183
SVIRSKY	Sarale	F					183
SVIRSKY	Chaia	F					183
SVIRSKY	Elyakim	M					183
SVIRSKY	Barukh	M					183
SVIRSKY	Simeh	F				2 children	183
SVIRSKY	Mordekhai Aizik	M				Married	183
SVIRSKY	Unknown	F			Mordechai Aizik	Married	183
SVIRSKY	Moshe	M					183
SOTZKEVER	Chaim	M					183
SOTZKEVER	Tziril	F					183
SOTZKEVER	Moshe Yitzhak	M					183
SIDARISKY	Yente Malke	F					183
SIDARISKY	Shepsel	M					183
SIDARISKY	Nehama Tzerneh	F					183
SIDARISKY	Libbe	F					183
SIDARISKY	Hiyeneh	F					183
SIDARISKY	Shlomo	M					183
SIDARISKY	Lea Reizl	F					183
SIDARISKY	Asher	M					183
SIDARISKY	Vikhne	F					183
SIDARISKY	Chaim Eliyahu	M					183
SIDARISKY	Esther	F					183
SIDARISKY	Badaneh	F					183
SIDARISKY	Bendet	M					183
STRIPONSKY	Berl	M				Married	183

STRIPONSKY	Unknown	F			Berl	Married	183
SPECTOR	Shmuel Yosef	M					183
SPECTOR	Sahrel	F					183
ע Ayin							return
ENGEL	Yosef	M					183
ENGEL	Rivka	F					183
ENGEL	Beilinkeh	F					183
ENGEL	Shmuel	M					183
EPSTEIN	Avraham	M					183
EPSTEIN	Chaia Diteh	F					183
EPSTEIN	Shimon	M					183
EPSTEIN	Devora	F				3 children	183
EPSTEIN	Eliyahu	M					183
EPSTEIN	Hasya	F				and family	184
EKMAN	Meir Aharon	M					184
EKMAN	Chana	F				3 children	184
פ Peh							
POTASHNIK	Bentzye	M					184
POTASHNIK	Shprintze	F					184
POTASHNIK	Chaim	M					184
POTASHNIK	Shmuel Yosef	M					184
POTASHNIK	Dabl	F				2 children	184
POTASHNIK	Noimeh	F					184
POTASHNIK	Dina	F					184
POTASHNIK	Shaul	M					184
POTASHNIK	Shepsel	M					184
POTASHNIK	Khiyeneh	F					184
POTASHNIK	Catriel	M					184
POTASHNIK	Glukeh	F					184
POTASHNIK	Zeldeh	F					184
POTASHNIK	Yitzhak	M					184
POTASHNIK	Unknown	F				Young girl	184
POTASHNIK	Laibe	M					184
POTASHNIK	Devora	F					184
POTASHNIK	Rahele	F					184
POTASHNIK	Shalom	M					184
POTASHNIK	Shulamit	F					184
POTASHNIK	Unknown	F				Young girl	184
POTASHNIK	Sara Elke	F					184
POTASHNIK	Chaia Tsherne	F					184
FISCHER	Zalman Mikhal	M					184

FISCHER	Yidel	M					184
FISCHER	Zlateh	F					184
FISCHER	Moshele	M					184
FISCHER	Chaim Avraham	M					184
FISCHER	Rahel	F					184
FISCHER	Malka	F					184
FISCHER	Velvel	M					184
FISCHER	Hirshel	M					184
FISCHER	Mikhal	M					184
FISCHER	Chana	F					184
FISCHER	Kvaleh	F					184
FISCHER	Freidel	F					184
FISCHER	Zalman Barukh	M					184
FISCHER	Unknown	F	Zalman Baruch				184
FISCHER	Shepsel	M					184
FISCHER	Rahel	F				Maiden name YUTER	184
FISCHER	Munyele	M					184
FISCHER	Chana Yasel	F					184
FISCHER	Shulamit	F					184
FISCHER	Munye	M					184
PEKING	Israel	M					184
PEKING	Ephraim	M					184
PEKING	Sara	F					184
PEKING	Hesye	F					184
PEKING	Unknown	F		Chesie			184
FRIEDSHON	Henekh	M					184
FRIEDSHON	Henye Feige	F					184
FRIEDSHON	Yehoshua	M					184

צ Tzadik

TZAKH	Isaac	M					184
TZAKH	Rayeh	F					184
TZAKH	Beileh	F					184
TZAKH	Yehoshua	M					185
TZAKH	Feiveh	F					185
TZAKH	Etel	F				2 children	185
TZAKH	Meir	M					185
TZARLANSKY	Yehuda Velvel	M					185
TZARLANSKY	Sara	F					185

TZARLANSKY	Rivka	F					185
TZARLANSKY	Yaakov	M				2 children	185
TZARLANSKY	Shalom Ehleh	M				and family	185
TZARLANSKY	Mattel	M					185
TZARLANSKY	Avigail	F					185
TZARLANSKY	Yehudit	F					185
TZARLANSKY	Yaakov	M					185
TZIRLIN	Leizer	M					185
TZIRLIN	Chana	F					185
TZIRLIN	Hirshel	M					185
TZIRLIN	Chaim	M					185
ק Kof							
KAMIN	Hava Dineh	F					185
KAMIN	Leizer	M					185
KAMIN	Henye	F					185
KAMIN	Yakhele	F					185
KAMIN	Esther	F					185
KAMIN	Unknown	F				Young girl	185
KAMIN	Shlomo Yitzhak	M					185
KAMIN	Eliyahu	M					185
KAMIN	Shifra	F					185
KAMIN	Hirsheh Leib	M					185
KAMIN	Beileh	F					185
KAMIN	Mikhal	M					185
KAMIN	Moshe	M					185
KAMIN	Meir Isaac	M					185
KAMIN	Simeh	F					185
KAGANOVITZ	Meir	M					185
KAGANOVITZ	Chana	F					185
KAGANOVITZ	Nehama	F					185
KAGANOVITZ	Gershon	M					185
KAPLAN	Henye	F					185
KAPLAN	Mordekhai Shimon	M					185
KAPLAN	Zeldeh	F				2 children	185
KARASIN	Mendel	M					185
KARASIN	Hirsheh	M					185
KARASIN	Hillel	M					185
KARASIN	Tzvia	F					185
KARASIN	Aharon	M					185
KARASIN	Taibl	F				2 children	185
KARPILEVSKY	Hirshel	M					185

KARPILEVSKY	Batya	F					185
KARPILEVSKY	Pesah	M				2 children	185
KOSZLOVITZ	Natte Getzel	M					185
KOSZLOVITZ	Ruhama	F					185
KOSZLOVITZ	Sara	F					185
KOSZLOVITZ	Mikhal	M				3 children	185
KISIN	Rasheh	F					185
KRAPIVNIK	Avrasha	M					186
KRAPIVNIK	Devora	F					186

ר Resh

RABINOVITZ	Eliyahu	M					186
RABINOVITZ	Chaia	F					186
RABINOVITZ	Hirshel	M					186
RABINOVITZ	Abbeleh	M					186
RABINOVITZ	Shlomo	M					186
RABINOVITZ	Yente	F					186
RABINOVITZ	Zelig	M					186
RABINOVITZ	Zalman	M					186
RABINOVITZ	Nehama	F					186
RABINOVITZ	Eliyahu	M	Zalman				186
RABINOVITZ	Gittel	F					186
RABINOVITZ	Zalman	M	Eli				186
RABINOVITZ	Chaim	M	Eli				186
RABINOVITZ	Unknown	F				Young girl	186
RABINOVITZ	Freidel	F				and family	186
RABINOVITZ	Nehama	F					186
RABINOVITZ	Nattel	F					186
RABINOVITZ	Chaim Feitel	M	Are				186
RABINOVITZ	Vikhne	F				2 children	186
RABINOVITZ	Leibeh	F					186
RABINOVITZ	Rahel	F					186
RABINOVITZ	Bendet	M					186
RABINOVITZ	Kaileh	F					186
RABINOVITZ	Shlomo	M					186
RABINOVITZ	Yitzhak	M					186
RABINOVITZ	Kaileh	F					186
RABINOVITZ	Natte	M				Married	186
RABINOVITZ	Unknown	F		Nute	Married		186
RABINOVITZ	Unknown	F	Nute				186
RABINOVITZ	Itke Tshernes	F					186
RAVITCH	Berl Yaakov	M					186
RAVITCH	Chaia Batya	F					186
RAVITCH	Moshe	M				2 children	186

RAVITCH	Benyamin	M					186
RAVITCH	Malka	F				3 children	186
REZNIK	Kofiman						186
REZNIK	Rivka Hindeh	F					186
REZNIK	Yitzhak	M					186
REZNIK	Chana	F					186
REZNIK	Zlateh	M					186
REZNIK	Shmuel	M					186
REZNIK	Rivka	F					186
REZNIK	Israel	M					186
REZNIK	Reuven Meir	M					186
REZNIK	Chaia	F					186
REZNIK	Dudel	M					186
REZNIK	Beileh	F					186
REZNIK	Chaim Yankel	M					186
REZNIK	Chaia	F					186
REZNIK	Rivka	F					186
REZNIK	Shlomo	M					186
REZNIK	Hiyeneh	F				2 children	186
REZNIK	Catriel	M					186
REZNIK	Aleksander	M				2 children	187
REZNIK	Chaim	M					187
REZNIK	Fanieh	F					187
REZNIK	Unknown	M				Young boy	187
REZNIK	Itche Avraham	M	Yitzhak				187
REZNIK	Sara	F					187
REZNIK	Dabbl	F					187
REZNIK	Henye	F				3 children	187
REZNIK	Shmuel Leibes	M					187
REZNIK	Reizl	F					187
REZNIK	Chaia Sara	F					187
REZNIK	Henye Eide	F					187
REZNIK	Leibele	M					187
RUBIN	Rivka Itel	F					187
ש Shin							
SHAYEVITZ	Avraham	M					187
SHAYEVITZ	Feige Rivka	F					187
SHAYEVITZ	Barukh Berl	M					187
SHAYEVITZ	Rahel	F				3 children	187
SHAYEVITZ	Feiveh	M					187

SHAYEVITZ	Rivka	F				3 children	187
SHAYEVITZ	Hillel	M					187
SHAYEVITZ	Menuha	F					187
SHAYKON	Mariashe	F					187
SHUSTER		F					187
SHOHET	Zelig	M					187
SHOHET	Dvosie	F				2 children	187
SHMERKOVITZ	Yaakov	M					187
SHMERKOVITZ	Batya	F					187
SHMERKOVITZ	Reuven Shneur	M					187
SHNEIDEROVITZ	Sheineh	F					187
SHNEIDEROVITZ	Beileh	F					187
SHNEIDEROVITZ	Sasheh	M					187
SHNEIDEROVITZ	Azon	M					187
SHAPIRA	Chaim	M					187
SHAPIRA	Zalman	M					187
SHAPIRA	Yaakov	M					187
SHREIDER	Daniel	M					187
SHREIDER	Hindeh	F					187
SHREIDER	Avraham	M					187

[Page 191]

Chapter Six

The Svirer in America and Other Lands

Matityahu Bogdanov
Avrum Chayat (Abraham)
Melekh Levin
Aharon Khoury **(Aaron)**

Svirer Social and Aid Association in America

Compiled on the basis of articles and letters written by the above-mentioned friends

Translated by Mindle Crystel Gross

The history of the Svir landslayt in America has now spanned almost 60 years. At the end of the 19th century, young Svir people already came to America. One of them was Melekh Levin, Yerakhmiyel and Gitl Levin's son. He arrived in America in 1899. His wife, Slaveh, Mirl Ayzikovitch's sister, was one of the first from Svir. Slowly, Svir began to move and a significant number of landslayt from our small town were in the U.S. by 1905. After the failure of the well-known Russian revolution, many from Svir fled to America who had been revolutionaries, who feared their being arrested and chased to imprisonment in Siberia. Among them were the dental technician Yankev Droyn and his bride, the Svir midwife, Lenye.

The Svir landslayt have spread far and wide throughout America, and even reached to Los Angeles and San Francisco in California. A large number settled in New York, and they were actually the first initiators in founding a committee of the Svir landslayt.

In truth, the Svir landdslayt had already begun to organize right after WWI. As it is told, for instance, Melekh Levin, right after WWI, visited his landslayt in Boston and there collected $800 to give help to the suffering and poor Jewish population in Svir. In that year, the Svir landslayt sent via a special messenger, $3500 to Svir.

This was, however, only a small beginning. In truth, the help from America was much larger, because each Svirer in America helped his own family in Svir to a great extent, and with money and with packages. This was the best indication, that the Svir landslayt had not forgotten their old home.

And so tens of years passed until WWII broke out and decimated almost all of Europe.

This influenced the Svir landslayt in America to organize officially as a social and aid organization.

The founder and initiator of the organization was Abraham Chayet, himself a son of parents of modest means, who suffered greatly in his life, and who felt a need to help the Jews of the old home.

In his letter to the friends in the State of Israel, he describes how even as a young boy of eight, he helped his parents to earn a little money. Even as a young child, he was active in collecting for food and benevolent matters, and so it was no wonder that with the onset of Hitler's storm, he immediately knocked on doors and asked for help for the needy in the distant old home.

This was following the holidays in 1939, a Sunday, when Abraham Chayet went to Heves Sudarski and explained his plan, that it was necessary to found a Svir aid society.

Sudarski did not need much convincing and the two of them quickly went to Yerukhmiyel, Borukh Ruven's son. There they accidentally met Shepsl the butcher's son and two of Yerakhmiyel's sons and their wives. All were in agreement, and they immediately decided to call a meeting at Abraham Chayet's and there to lay the foundation of the Svir Society.

[Page 193]

**Aaron Khoury, President of the Svir Social
and Aid Society in America**

More people than expected came to the meeting. Everybody was happy that finally there was the possibility of doing something for the old home.

On November 26th, 1939, at 73 Ludlow Street in New York, there was a large meeting, with the chairman Morris Fisher. Philip Raz gave a report about the situation of the Svir Jews. Following the meeting, an administration was elected to whom the various responsibilities were delegated, as follows:

President: Morris Fisher
V.P.: Eva Raz
Treasurer: Harry Levin
Fin. Sec.:" Nathan Greenberg
Protocol Sec. Max Bogdanov

The Svir landslayt were enthusiastic and were not stingy with either money or effort, so that the action should succeed. As Abraham Chayet describes in his letter, he came to take a check from Yankev Hirsh, Yerakhmiyel's son, and Yankev Hirsh explained to him, that this was the greatest day of his life when he can participate in such a holy cause, to send help to Svir Jews.

During the years, the presidents of the Society changed, but the work was always continued with love and concern.

[Page 194]

Melekh Levin and his wife

It is worthwhile mentioning that the first president was Morris Fisher, the second – Louis Ayzikson, Shepsl the butcher's son-in-law, and the third – Aaron Khoury, Borukhthe teacher's son, who has held the position from 1943, for almost 15 years.

[Page 195]

**Blume Chayet, of blessed memory,
and Aaron Chayet**

Abraham Chayet writes:

Aaron Khoury infused new life into the Society. He himself donated large amounts of money and influenced others to do the same.

As we said, Aaron Khoury took over the position in December, 1943. When he received the terrible news about the barbaric deeds of the Hitlerists, he immediately sent out a call, saying that the tragedy is huge and the aid work must begin immediately and on a grand scale. And his appeal really helped. In one evening there was collected $2000. He was the first one to give $100 and the others did not hold back. It is interesting that for a Hanukah evening, the charge was $200 for the honor of making blessings and to light the Hanukah candles. Aaron Khoury related in a letter about the colossal work of the administration:

"We did not miss anyone from Svir, no matter where he was. We wrote, we called, we visited and traveled. A separate chore was to find who of the Svir remained, where they were and what we could do for them. We contacted the United Jewish Appeal and HIAS.

[Page 196]

**Yakov Drutz of blessed memory,
died in Los Angeles**

In addition, we also had to help various aged and sick Svirer who are in America.

"All of this colossal work was done by Libby Gold and me. It gave us great satisfaction to do this work".

In addition to the aid the American friends gave the needy from Svir in America and Europe, they joined the Svir Society in Israel, and sent aid and money and even packages. Thanks to this, the Svir Benevolent Society was founded in Israel, and this will also help in printing this book about Svir. Svirer in America are also active in various other institutions and organization and help out with collecting funds for undertakings of the Israeli government and the Zionist movement.

The Svirer in the entire world will read about this with great joy and pride, and will send their friends in America a hearty thank-you.

[Page 198]

List of Active Members of the Svir Organization in New York

(Their function in the organization and years of activity)

(Member = member of the executive committee)

Translated by Yocheved Klausner

Surname	Name	Name of father	Activity & Years	Remarks
ISAKSOHN	Louis		member 1940 president 1941-44 member 1945-1958	father-in-law Shebsl [Shabtay] was a butcher
ISAKSOHN	Sarah	Shebsl [Shabtay]	member 1940, 1945-1958	father was a butcher
ITZKOWITZ	Morris		member 1939	
ITZKOWITZ	Rose	Slave	member 1940	father was a tailor
BOGDANOV	Max	Matityahu	secretary 1939-1940 member 1941 vice-president 1945-1958	
GOLD	Liebe		financial secretary 1942-1956	mother's name Sara Riva
GREENBERG	Isaac z"l	Eliyahu	member 1939 until his death	father was a carpenter
GREENBERG	Nathan		financial secretary member 1939-1941	grandfather Eliyahu was a carpenter
DEUTCH	Dara		member 1940-1944	mother's name Hinde Chaia
CHAYAT	Abraham	Yosef	member 1939, treasurer 1940 vice-president 1941 member 1942-1956 financial secretary 1957	
CHAYAT	Bluma z"l		member 1945 until her death	wife of Abraham Chayat
CHAYAT	Harry z"l	Yosef	member 1939-1940 vice-president 1942-1944 member 1945 until his death	
TINKOFF	Ray (Rivka)	Shebsl [Shabtay]		father was a butcher
LEVINE	Harry z"l	Yerachmiel	treasurer 1939	Hebrew name Yosef Hirshel
LEVINE	Judith z"l		member 1945 until her death	

Surname	Name	Name of father	Activity & Years	Remarks
LEVINE	Max	Yerachmiel	treasurer 1945-1958	
LEVINE	Eddy z"l	Yerachmiel	member 1939 until his death	Hebrew name Refael
MILLER	Alex		member 1939-1944	
SOLOW	Joseph z"l		secretary 1942 until his death	
SWIRSKI	Philip		member 1939	
SIDARSKI	Harry		member 1939-1958	mother's name Chava Yente Malka
SIDARSKI	Sarah		member 1945-1958	

[Page 199]

Surname	Name	Name of father	Activity & Years	Remarks
PATOSHNIK	Avraham	Moshe Itze	member 1939 secretary 1941	
FISCHER	Herman	Avraham Zelig	member 1939	
FISCHER	Morris	Shebsl [Shabtay]	president 1939-1940	father was a butcher member 1941-1958
FISCHER	Sadie z"l	Chaim Yudel	member 1941-1958	mother's name Sara Tzirl
KORY	Aharon	Baruch	treasurer 1941-1944 president 1945-1958	former name KURITZKI
KORY	Ida		member 1945-1958	
RAZ	Eva	Shebsl [Shabtay]	vice-president 1939 member 1940-1958	father was a butcher
SCHNEIDER	Abe		member 1940-1944	

List of Former Residents of Svir in America
who have participated in
the
"Svir Social and Help Organization" in New-York

Translated by Yocheved Klausner

Surname	First name
ISAKSOHN	Louie
ISAKSOHN	Sarah
ITZKOWITZ	Morris
ABRAHAMS	Yakov
ABRAHAMS	
BUCK	Hyman
BOGDANOV	Max
BRESLAV	M.
BROMBERG	Gussie
BRESLAV	Al.
GLASSER	N.
GABSTEIN	Y.
GABSTEIN	Anna
GOLD	Liebe
GOLD	B.Z.
GORDON	Sarah
GREENBERG	Harry
GREENBERG	M.
GREENBERG	Isac z"l
GREENBERG	I.K.
GREENBERG	Nathan
GRASS	Abraham
DEUTCH	Dora
DEUTCH	Sofie
HEILPERN	Julius
HARRISON	Max
HARRISON	Lilian
HOFFMAN	Al.
HOFFMAN	Sam
HOFFMAN	Simon
HOROWITZ	Mars.
WEINER	Harry

Surname	First name
WEINSTEIN	Esther
WEINSTEIN	Sam
WEINSTEIN	H.
WEINSTEIN	Rose
WELLER	Lea
CHAYAT	Blume z"l

[Page 200]

Surname	First name
CHAYAT	Avraham
CHAYAT	Harry z"l
TISCHMANN	Fany
TYNKOFF	Rivka
COHEN	Heyman
LERNER	Yosef
LEVINE	Edward z"l
LEVINE	Julia
LEVINE	Harry z"l
LEVINE	Max
LEVINE	R.
LEVINE	Anna
LIEBER	Eva
MELZER	Bella
METZ	Max
METZ	Esther
MILLER	Alex
MILLER	Fany
MILLER	Ida
MILLER	Sam
SWIRSKI	Sam
SYKEN	Eve
SWIRSKI	Philip
SIDARSKI	Abe
SIDARSKI	P.
SIDARSKI	Harry
SIDARSKI	Sarah
SIDARSKI	Morris
SOLOW	Yosef z"l
SWYER	Nathan
SENDERS	P.

EPSTEIN	Yeta
FINN	Dr. Mania
FISCHER	Herman
FISCHER	Y.
FISCHER	Yakov
FISCHER	Julius
FISCHER	Sadie z"l
FISCHER	Morris
FISCHER	Sol
FRIEDMAN	B.
FALK	M.
FRIEDMAN	Sam
FISCHER	Dr. Michael
FALSTEIN	Ch.
FALSTEIN	Y.
FALSTEIN	Julius
FINE	S.
PATOSH	Isidore
PATOSHNIK	Abraham
PATOMKIN	A.
KANTEROWITZ	Harry
KANTEROWITZ	Refael
KOPELOWITZ	Louis
KORY	Aharon
KORY	Ida
RABINOWITZ	R.
ROGOZIN	Fany
ROSEE	Eva
ROSEE	Philip
SHEYKON	Y.
SHULMAN	Bella
SHULMAN	Bessie
SHULMAN	Y.
STERN	Bella
SCHNEIDER	Abe
SCHWARTZ	Sol
SCHWARTZ	Sadie
SCHWARTZ	Walter
SHERMAN	W.
SCHWARTZ	Shmuel Yakov

List of Former Residents of Svir in America
who have participated in the
"Svir Social and Help Organization" in New-York

Translated by Yocheved Klausner

Surname	First name	Father's name
YOEL (FISCHER)	Gutl	Zalman Baruch
YOEL	Zalman Baruch	Welwel
MINDEL	Abe	Yosef
MECHNOWITZ	Baruch	Avraham Yitzhak
MELZER	Yitzhak	Chaim
MELZER (FISCHER)	Tzirl z"l	Zalman Baruch
MARKS (MELZER)	Chaia	Yitzhak
FISCHER	Yitzhak	Zalman Baruch
FISCHER	Bashel	
FISCHER	Henie	Yitzhak
FISCHER	Zalman Baruch	Yitzhak
REZNIK	Avraham	Leib
STERN (MELZER)	Reiche	Yitzhak

In France

Surname	First name	Father's name
ALPEROWITZ	Berl	Chaim
RABINOWITZ-ALPEROWITZ	Yehudit	Bendet
ZLATAYAVKA	Shabad Sheine	Baruch Berl

In Cuba

Surname	First name	Father's name
ZLATAYAWSKI	Zalman	Baruch Berl
KORITZKI	Hirshel	Baruch
KOPELOWITZ	Yakov Moshe	

[Page 202]

In Germany

Surname	First name	Father's name
CHAYAT	David	Reuven
CHAYAT-JAFFE	Reizl	Reuven
DREWIATZKI	Chaia Tzipa	Moshe
DREWIATZKI	Mordchai	Moshe
JAFFE	Aizik	David-Ber
SWIRSKI-DREWIATZKI	Pessie	Elyakum

In Russia and Poland

Surname	First name	Father's name
BUSHKANETZ	Shmuel	Yakov
GERSHOWITZ-SWIRSKI	Ita	Israel
DIMENSTEIN-YOEL	Fruma	Avraham-Hirsh
CHADASH	called *Der Kriwitzer*	
CHADASH	Chana	Meir
YANKELEVITZ	Hirshel	Bendet
MOLLER	Fruma	Eliyahu
MECHNOWITZ	Feige	Shimon Eliyahu
MECHNOWITZ	Zelde	Shimon Eliyahu
MILLNER	Yakov	Ben-Zion
PATOSHNIK	Leib	Israel
PEKING	Esther	Israel
SOLOMYAK	Yerachmiel	Bere Yankel
SOLOMYAK	Batia	Yerachmiel
SWIRSKI		
SWIRSKI		
SWIRSKI		
KAPLAN	Avraham	Hirsh
SCHREIDER	Nachum	Avraham

In Uruguay

Surname	First name	Father's name
BUSHKANETZ-ZLATAYAWKA	Sprintze	Yakov
BUSHKANETZ	Moshe	Yakov
BUSHKANETZ	Rachel	Yakov
GORDON	Rivka	
GORDON	Sara	Israel
GORDON	Idel	Israel
SWIRSKI-BUSHKANETZ	Esther	Eliyahu-Nathan
SWIRSKI	Reizl	Meir Zelig

In Brazil

Surname	First name	Father's name
AIZIKOWITZ-SWIRSKI	Fradl	Mechl
BARCHANOWITZ	Liebe	Chaim
KATZ	Yitzhkak	Shlomo
KATZ	Yosef	Shlomo
KATZ	Lea	Shlomo
KATZ	Chaia	Shlomo
SWIRSKI	Manie	Aharon

In Canada

Surname	First name	Father's name
WEILER	Rachel	Shimon Leizer
WEILER	Berl	Shimon Leizer
WEILER	Baruch	Shimon Leizer
WEILER	Lollie	Shimon Leizer
KAPLAN	Fere	Hirshl
DIMENSTEIN	Rivka	Avraham Hirsh

[Page 204]

In Argentina

Surname	First name	Father's name
ABEL	Meitzik	Tuvia
SWIRSKI	Lieber	Elyakim
SWIRSKI	Sara	Peretz
SOLOMIAK	Avraham Yitzhak	Yerachmiel
SOLOMIAK	Niriam	Mordechai
KAMIN	Yosef	Meir Itzik
KAMIN	Shmerl	Meir Itzik
KAMIN	Yehoshua	Meir Itzik
KAMIN	Sara	Meir Itzik
RAZOLER	Shimon	
	Shalom (called Shalom from Spiale)	

Seder Pesah [Passover meal] at the Fine family, daughter of Feive Swirski, Berlin 1929

[Page 207]

The Svirer in the Land of Israel

At the Annual Svir Gathering

Shmuel Dobkin

Translated by Yocheved Klausner

We have again gathered, to hold the annual meeting of all the Svir Landsleit [former Jewish residents] who are now living here in Israel.

It is obvious that we would want to meet – we, the few who were left of Svir – to chat, to discuss our common concerns, to remember everything and everyone.

However, as it is mentioned in the Talmud: had you been worthy, you would read the verse "**These** are the feasts of the Lord" [Leviticus 23:4]; now that you are not worthy, you read the verse "For **these** things I weep" [Lamentations 1:16]. This gathering should have been a gathering of joy and festivity, but unfortunately our memories make us weep.

The annual convention in Kfar Saba, 1952

[Page 208]

Had we been worthy and the horrible things had not happened, our gathering would have been a great celebration. The new immigrants would have brought us greetings from our home, and our hearts would have been filled with joy. Today, we are not more than a few remnants of our town; we listen to sad greetings and we remember our former home, which exists no more.

Where are the words that could describe the great tragedy that has befallen the town and the people? What expression could convey in a few short minutes our pain and sorrow for our dearest whom we have lost in such a tragic way? Perhaps the best form of expression would be total silence. A great writer once said: "The power of the silence between the words often says more than the words themselves."

As I stand now before you, to say a few words about our town, I remember a chapter from the book of the prophet Yehezkel [Ezekiel], which we shall read in the Torah Portion of this week.

This is the famous prophecy about the valley that was full of dry bones, which, by the command of God through the mouth of the prophet, "came together, were covered with flesh and skin" and became alive, standing up on their feet to form a great army. And God said to the prophet "These bones are the whole house of Yisrael."

[Page 209]

New immigrants from Svir in 1950

Dear friends, Svirer Jews! We do not have the divine power to bring to life the dry bones of our nearest and dearest. We do not have even the merit to know where their bones are scattered; but we do know that today, as we are gathered here, we can and we must remember them and always keep them alive in our memories.

Let us now, for a while, wander away together with our memories to our town, and behold our home of long ago, where Jewish souls are hovering and do not find rest; let us look at the times when we lived there, times of childhood and youth, times of suffering and happiness, times of a vigorous

[Page 210]

life in different domains – social, cultural and national. Let us, for a while, unite our thoughts with all this, remember and not forget.

And may our children learn from all this and may the memories remain with us forever.

Remember and do not forget! – This is what we say about our town. This is the candle that we light today for the memory of our old home!

The Svir Immigrants in Israel, Their Association and their Interest-Free Fund

Dov Yoel

Translated by Yocheved Klausner

1. Svirer in Israel

Thanks to the Zionist movement in Svir, to the pioneer education of the Svir Youth and to the Hebrew school, many Svir Jews made Aliya to Eretz Israel during the 20s of the 20th century, and the Aliya expanded during the 30s. In 1944, before the survivors of the Hitler gangs began to arrive, some 60 Svir families (in 12 of them both husband and wife were from Svir) lived throughout the country, in cities and towns, moshavim and kibbutzim. Most of them lived in Tel Aviv, Kfar Saba and kibbutz Ramat Rachel.

[Page 211]

The families kept in contact and visited each other during holidays or joyful events, but a formal Svir organization did not exist. Like all the other Jews in the country, we felt that we were part of the Yishuv [the Jewish settlement in Eretz Israel] and we did nor did we feel the need to create a special circle or organization of the Landsleit.

However, the situation changed after the Second World War, when new immigrants from Svir began to arrive. They needed advice and assistance in their attempts to create a new life for themselves, and it became necessary to establish an organization dedicated to that purpose. The Svirer Association exists since 1945.

The following numbers show the distribution of the Svir residents in Israel, according to profession, place of residence etc. In 1958 the number of families and unmarried persons reached 110.

The Svir immigrants in Israel in 1958

1. By dates of Aliya		3. By place of residence	
Before 1944	59 families	a. In cities:	
After 1944	45 families	Tel Aviv	18 families
Total	104	Jerusalem	5 families
		Haifa	2 families
2. By profession		Other cities	14 families
Merchants	25	**Total in cities**	39 families
Farmers	22		
Office workers	16	b. In towns:	
Artisans	11	Kfar Saba	25 families
Teachers	7	Other towns	15 families
Drivers	6	**Total in towns**	40 families
Contractors	2		
Manufacturers	2	c. In villages	13 families
Without profession	13	d. In kibbutzim	12 families
Total	104	**Total in Israel**	104 families

[Page 212]

2. The Association of the Svir Immigrants in Israel

In April 1945, when first bits of information about Svir and its Jews began to reach us, several of the veteran Svir immigrants met in Tel Aviv and created a "Temporary committee, with the purpose pf acquiring aid for the Svir Jews."

The members of the committee were:

Shmuel Blyacher – chairman
Shmuel Dobkin – secretary
Dov Yoel – treasurer
Hanoch (Henech) Drutz- Svironi, Moshe Yaffe, Ozer Miller – members

The aims of the committee were:

1. To collect information about Svir Jews who survived the war.
2. To get in touch with them and send help.
3. To collect any information available about those who perished.

At the beginning of our activity our financial means were quite limited, and the cost of the first packages of food and clothing that we sent out was kindly covered by the Association of the Svenchan Jews in Israel and by the Jewish Agency through the Association of the Vilna Jews.

I would like to extend special thanks to the chairman of the Svenchan group, our friend Heshel Gurewitz (from New-Svenchan) for the help he has sent to the Svir people.

Terrible and sad news began to arrive – that only very few of the Svir Jews survived. It was difficult to get in touch with them, and we were not sure whether the help we sent had reached them. But the Committee did not stop hoping that in time more survivors will show up, and it was imperative that we create the means to help them. We asked the Svir immigrants in Israel to send us donations, as well as any information they might receive about relatives and friends from Svir. In 1946 we contacted, through Mrs. Liebe Gold, the financial secretary of "The Svir Social Association" in New York,

[Page 213]

Mr. Aharon Kourie, the president of the Association. Thanks to the help of this organization we were able to expand our activities.

During the next few years, we received information about Jews from Svir and the surrounding villages and towns who had survived and were scattered in the camps in Germany, France and other countries, on their way to Eretz Israel.

We included in our active team our friends from Kfar Saba: Heshel Miller, Gershon Yoel, Sara Tzach and Yosef Desyatnik. We planned to convene a meeting of all the Svir immigrants in Israel, however due to the events of 1947 and the War of Independence in 1948 we had to postpone the plan. In the meantime, the first immigrants arrived and we sought to help them in various ways: our money sources were limited (for 100 dollars, sent by the American organization, we received only 35 Israeli pounds; in one year we received about 500 dollars), so that the sum we could give any immigrant at arrival was low – more like a small "welcoming gift" rather than real help; but we did assist them by other means, in their first steps in the new land: we used our influence to obtain for the new immigrants a loan from the bank and helped with the guarantee, and we helped them find work and a place to live.

When we located the veteran Svir immigrants in the country, we found out that not all of them were well off and had regular work; some of them were badly in need of help.

The tasks of the organization multiplied, and we felt the need to create a stronger

[Page 214]

Svir organization, and to bring together the Svir veterans with the newly arrived. This way we could not only listen to the new immigrants and receive a direct account of the fate of our parents, brothers and sisters, but also create for them a warm and pleasant environment, in addition to our efforts to help them find work and dwellings.

The first annual convention of the former Svir residents was held in 1949 in Kfar Saba, where a large number of Svir families lived. About 60 people from all over the country attended, among them about 20 new immigrants. Some came with their families.

It is difficult to express the situation, and the excitement of all present: the meeting between the older residents in Israel, who had not seen each other in 10-20 years and, more than that, the meeting with the few survivors.

The official agenda of the convention was:

    1.   A memorial service for the Svir martyrs and for the Svir children fallen in the War of Independence.
    2.   Welcoming greetings to the newly arrived.
    3.   A prayer for the wounded in the war.
    4.   A few words about our town Svir: The story of the downfall of the Svir Jewish community, as told by the new immigrants.
    5.   A report by the Temporary Committee about the accomplishments from 1945 to 1949, and the relations with the Svirer Association in America and the help it has extended.
    6.   Election of a Council and Board of Directors of the Association.

The official part of the convention created a sad atmosphere. Of the 900-1,000 Jews who lived in Svir before the war very few survived – only 125-150 souls, according to the information we had. About 50 of them came to

[Page 215]

Israel or were on the way, the others were still in the refugee camps and planned to go to America or to other countries. Very few remained in Svir.

The listeners broke out in tears when Henech Drutz spoke about "Our little town Svir" and said: This meeting is like a memorial service, where all the orphans gathered to recite the Kadish.

We all sat, petrified, when the newcomers Berl, Chasye and Zalman Reznik described shortly the long story of pain, persecution, hunger and murder against the Jewish population.

The discussions continued until late at night and it was felt that such meetings should be convened in the next years as well. A council of 13 members was elected; six of them were chosen to form the Board of Directors. The convention made the following decisions:

1. To contact all the former Svir residents around the world.
2. To establish assistance funds.
3. To collect material about the Svir community and publish a book.
4. To organize a convention at least once a year.

Until the year 1956, every year a convention was held (we had 8 annual conventions). The agenda of each convention was:

1. The report of the Board of Directors and new elections.
2. Stories and memories from the old home, told by the participants.

The number of the participants increased each year and at times reached 100 adults. Several times we hired a photographer, to preserve the moments of the meetings.

In October 1953, we called a special meeting of the Svir former residents in

[Page 216]

Israel, in honor of our friend from America Bluma Chayat z"l and her husband Avraham Chaim – both very capable workers of the Svir Association in America. Mrs. Chayat was not originally from Svir, but she was a great help to her husband in his devoted and wholehearted work for the Svirer in America and Israel.

We could not organize a convention in the years 1957 and 1958, for several reasons. We are planning to resume the conventions with the appearance of the Svir book.

The daily work of the association is carried out by the board of directors, which works as an executive committee. It consists of 6 members. The full council of 13 members meets once or twice a year, to discuss the general matters concerning the association.

Although the board of directors presented its report to the Convention every year, it is interesting to compare the following financial report with the regular activities during the last 13 years:

1. A welcoming gift for every immigrant at arrival to the country (1-30 pounds).
2. Assistance in money and packages.
3. Help in finding work and dwelling, & presents on joyful occasions.
4. Help in receiving loans through the bank, including guarantees.
5. Preparations for the publication of the Svir Book: collecting material, printing the material on a typewriter, collecting photographs etc., and finally printing the book.
6. Expenses for conventions, mail etc.

The Svir immigrants in Israel participated in the current expenses of the association. But without the help of our friends in America we would not have been able to realize all the projects of our organization and establish the interest-free loan fund. And although we are aware of the fact that several of our friends have for years "pulled the wagon" I would like to mention in particular our friend

[Page 217]

Aharon Kourie, with whom we have been corresponding during the 13 years of our activity. In addition to his work for the association year by year, he has personally contributed large sums to the Svir association, and lately he sent a large sum for the publication of the book (which is not mentioned in the following report). To Aharon Kourie and the others who are active in the association we send our heartfelt thanks.

General Report of Income and Expenses 1945-1957

Income		Expenses	
From the association in America (not including the loan-fund			
For help	860	For help	950
For the book	360	Preparation of book	340
Total	1220	Conventions, office expenses etc.	230
		Total	1520
From Svirer in Israel			
For current expenses, preparation of book, help	650	In the bank, account of the book	730
Book	380		
	1030		
Total	2250	Total	2250

The above report does not include the income and expenses
of the published book "Our Shtetl Svir"

[Page 218]

The Council and the Board of Directors

1. Dov Yoel – president
2. Heshel Miller – vice-president
3. Shmuel Dobkin – secretary
4. Moshe Yaffe – treasurer
5. Gershon Yoel – member
6. Yosef Desyatnik – member
7. Shmuel Blyacher
8. Chanoch Drutz
9. Herzl Weiner
10. Yitzhak Fischer
11. Sara Tzach-Chayat
12. Zalman Reznik

3. The Svir Interest-Free Loan Fund

The Fund for interest-free loan, in the name and memory of the martyrs of the Jewish community of Svir (near Vilna)

Established by the former residents of Svir in the USA and Israel
192 Arlozorov St. Tel Aviv, c/o Yoel

In 1953, the board of directors of the Svir association decided to create a loan fund without interest [*Gemilut Chasadim*, lit. "bestowing charity"], which would serve as a constructive help for the immigrants from Svir who needed a loan. The first 200 pounds for this purpose were donated by Sol Schwarz (son of Aharon Schwarzgar) and his wife, and another 100 pounds – by Blume and Avraham Chayat, Svir immigrants in America who visited Israel at that time. We send them our heartfelt thanks.

When the Svir association in America received, through Avraham Chayat, a detailed report about our activity and our plan to create an interest-free loan fund, they sent us at the beginning of 1954 the sum of 2350 pounds and by the end of 1957 another 1700 pounds.

In 1954, we duly registered our association with the authorities, and the loan fund became an official social project. Six members of the council were elected to serve as founders and members of the executive committee of the fund, and they are managing the fund to this day (see the exact list at the end of this article).

[Page 219]

It was decided to register all the Svir immigrants as members of the fund organization. The enrolling fee was the very low sum of half a pound.

The functions of the fund: to extend loans to any member, in the cases where help was truly needed for practical and productive objectives, under the following conditions:

1. The loan will be returned by monthly installments, by the decision of the board of directors.
2. The borrower will not pay interest, in any form.
3. As guarantee, the Fund will receive a promissory note signed by the borrower. The guarantors will be his wife and two other residents.

Even before the official opening of the Fund's activity, several applications for loans were received, which proved that the project was a real necessity at the time.

During the first years of the existence of the Fund we gave out loans of 100 to 200 pounds; in the last few years we raised the amounts to 200 pounds. The monthly return payments were 10 pounds, and in difficult cases 5 pounds.

In a separate list we present the distribution of the loans by years and amounts. We note with satisfaction, that all the loans have been returned on time.

I think it would be interesting to know how the Fund is functioning. Our working principle is: to make the least difficulties for our members, to spare expenses and to authorize the loan as soon as possible.

Since the Svirer live in all parts of the country, they submit their requests for a loan by mail. The board of directors meets to discuss the request, or, in urgent cases, the entire procedure is carried out through the mail: the president obtains the approval of the other members, the decision is sent to the candidate for the

[Page 220]

loan and the latter sends back by mail the guarantee, signed by himself and by the guarantors. The loan is received by the borrower at the post office (the Post Bank). The monthly payments are made through the Post Bank as well and all the administrative fees are paid by the Fund, so that burden on the borrower and his guarantors, regarding cost and effort, is kept to a strict minimum. Moreover, unlike other financial institutions, we do not demand that the borrower and the guarantors sign the guarantee in the presence of a member of our board of directors; they may sign it in the presence of one of the councilmen in their place of residence and, after the signatures are confirmed by the councilman, send it to us by mail.

Compared to other similar funds, which carry out their transactions through regular banks, we think that ours is a very efficient and cost-effective arrangement.

[Page 221]

Distribution of loans

1. According to years and amounts (in Israeli pounds)

Up until	Amount	Total		
	Up to 100	Over 100	Loans	Amounts
1. 30 Sept. 1954	1	2	3	400
2. 30 Sept. 1955		14	14	2100
3. 30 Sept. 1956	1	13	14	2050
4. 30 Sept. 1957		13	13	2250
Total	2	42	44	6800

2. According to occupations (in the above mentioned years)

Year	Artisans		Laborers		Grocers		Farmers		Clerks		Lib. Prof.	
	No.	Amount	No.	Amount	No.	Amount	No.	Amount	No.	Amount	No.	Amount
1	2	300	1	100								
2	1	150	2	300	2	300	4	600	4	600	1	150
3	3	400	2	300	2	300	3	450	2	300	2	300
4	4	650			3	450	2	350	2	450	2	350
Total	10	1500	5	700	7	1050	9	1400	8	1350	5	800

3. According to Goals

Number	Goals	Amount
8	For an apartment in a housing project	1300
5	For changes in apartment/adding rooms	750
7	For apartments and children's weddings	1050
8	Cleaning	1150
8	For business	1300

4	For farming	600
1	For locksmith machinery	150
2	For health purposes	300
1	For trip to America, (son's study)	200
44 loans	Israeli Pounds	6800

[Page 222]

Financial Report of the Fund – 1953-1957

Income:

From the Society in New York	4050 Pounds
From Sol Schwartz	200
From Avraham Chayat	100
From Dov Resnik	10
Membership fees	32
Bank interest	8
Total	**4400 Pounds**

Expenses

For defense fund (*keren magen*)	40
Founding expenses, stamps and other office expenses	120
Total	**160 Pounds**
Debts on loans	1875
	2035
In the bank	2365
	4400

The Board of Directors of the Fund since 1953:

Dov Yoel – president and book-keeper
Heshel Miller – vice-president
Yitzhak Fischer – secretary
Shmuel Dobkin – treasurer
Yosef Desyatnik – member
Moshe Yaffe – member
Gershon Yoel - member

[Page 223]

We have described in detail the activity of our Society and Fund and have presented the financial reports, hoping that our friends in America and in Israel are assured that their contributions have helped – in various ways – the Svir landsleit, that the amounts of money were distributed rationally, and that the administration expenses were kept to a minimum.

Lastly, it is worth mentioning that, compared to the other towns, the Svir Society is very well-organized, and our daily work is carried out in friendly co-operation of all Svir former residents, here in Israel as well as in America.

May this serve as a measure of consolation to us in the great sorrow after the destruction of our old home, and the murderous cleansing of our nearest and dearest.

The administration of the Svir Society in Israel:

Seated from right to left: S. Dobkin, Y. Fisher, D. Yoel, H. Miller and H. Weiner
Y. Desyatnik, H. Drutz-Svironi, Sh. Chayat, Z. Resnik and G. Yoel

[Page 224]

The Svirer in Eretz Israel

Dr. Chanoch Swironi

Translated by Yocheved Klausner

Svir was considered a Zionist town. In every family, at least one of the members of the family aspired to make Aliya to Eretz Israel. Right after the WWI, the first who began the journey was the old Shochet [slaughterer] R'Tzadok. He did not, however, go to live in Eretz Israel, but to fulfill the wish to die in the Holy Land. Some time later, the Rabbi and Talmud teacher R'Moshe Aharon Schwarzgar and his wife Shoshe made Aliya to Eretz Israel for the same purpose.

The first Svirer who went to Eretz Israel to create there a new life for himself and his family was Sinai Kutcher. All his acquaintances felt sorry for him and criticized him; some tried to dissuade him saying that all those who went there came back. What will you eat? – argued the neighbors – perhaps the stones, the rocks or the sand… Some of the "good friends" even laughed at him and spread jokes: At the most you will have the opportunity to ride a camel… Only one, Henech Zlatayavke, reassured him and said, before he bade him farewell:

"You go, Sinai, and open a wide road for all the others." Indeed he went – it was the year 1924 – but on his way he met many who were on their way back and they simply mocked him. But he did not let this deter him.

Since he had very little money to spend on this voyage, he went on a cargo ship, and after six weeks of a difficult journey and much distress he arrived at the port of Yafo [Jaffa].

[Page 225]

During the first year, Sinai did not enjoy much of the "milk and honey" of the land. He worked hard, and his salary was paid by "food-notes" instead of money. Yet, he managed to overcome the hardships through the first difficult years and he sent for his wife and children.

The farewell wish of Henech Zlatayavke, however, came true: a broad path was opened, and Svir people began to come.

Moshe Aharon and Shoshe Schwarzgar z"l

In town, the *Hechalutz* movement was organized, and when the first "certificate" was received, it was clear that it must go to the president of *Hechalutz*, Chaim Chayat. He registered Reizl Chazan as his wife – and this was the first pioneer Aliya from Svir. A great farewell party was arranged for the couple, the town youth escorted them to the bridge and enthusiastic goodbyes were exchanged.

Some time later, the woman pioneer Chaia Kuritzki, registered for Aliya. She was criticized and ridiculed. If you want to work hard and cut stones, there are enough stones in Kremenets, they said.

[Page 226]

But all these warnings did not help. The youth did not pay attention to them, and tens of *Hechalutz* members, young men and women, prepared for Aliya, despite the difficulties. The problem was how to obtain "aliya certificates" for all of them.

After Chaia Kuritzki, the next young people who emigrated were Avraham Yitzak Miller, Shlomo Kalman Blyacher with his family, Binyamin Kamin and Sheine Miller and Chanan Gendel with his family. Svir began to wake up. Sinai has indeed opened a wide path for all others.

In time, the Svir Jews became accustomed to the *Chalutzim* [pioneers] Aliya. It came to be regarded as a natural occurrence in town – until the outbreak of the 1929 riots in Eretz Israel. The August 1929 events left a very painful impression in Svir. Mourning assemblies were organized and a memorial service for the murdered was held in the *Bet Hamidrash*. Yitzhak Ben-Tzvi, the chairman of the *Vaad Leumi* [National Committee] in Eretz Israel, sent a telegram to the Jews over the world asking for urgent help. When the telegram reached Svir, the people understood that this time it was not a question of sending a few Zloty. The *Hechalutz* committee held several meetings and it was decided to send immediately 5 *chalutzim* to

Eretz Israel. They were: Heshel Miller, Gershon Yoel, Yitzhak Fischer, Shlomo Chodesh and Sara Lea Potashnik.

On the eve of their departure, a festive banquet was organized. The most respected people in town gathered to the farewell party, and spoke with admiration about the five *chalutzim*. All felt that this time Svir was participating in an entirely different

[Page 227]

way in the struggle for Eretz Israel.

In the course of the evening, the Rabbi, Aba Berkman, suddenly arrived and asked to say a few words. The news spread in town like fire, that the rabbi himself came to bide farewell to the pioneers. A large crowd gathered around the place, and in respectful silence they listened to the rabbi's speech.

Baruch Kuritzki z"l

The rabbi spoke about Eretz Israel, about the eternal bond between Eretz Israel and the Jewish people, about Jewish heroes in the past and today and about the wars of the Hasmoneans. How great was the surprise when the rabbi began to read a poem by the Hebrew poet Chaim Nachman Bialik, *Im yesh et nafshecha ladaat* [If you wish to know], reciting slowly and translating line by line to Yiddish.

[Page 228]

Our great national poet, said the rabbi, asked the following question in his famous poem: "From where did the Jewish nation draw the strength and the endurance to withstand such suffering? From which source did they draw the courage to leap alive into the fire and not abandon their faith? Where did they find consolation and comfort in their pain"? To all these questions Bialik replied – a reply that was to become famous:

Go to the old Bet Hamidrash [synagogue, lit: house of learning].

Come in to the old Bet Hamidrash, there you will find the wonderful fresh spring.

But now – Rabbi Berkman raised his voice – when someone will come today and ask where do the Jews find the strength and courage to withstand the Arab attacks, we must modify Bialik's answer and say that here, in this place where we are now, I see the amazing spring, the true source. So long as the Jewish nation possesses pioneers such as these five, who are about to step directly into the fire, without fear or hesitation, with passion, driven by an inner force, so long as we have such a youth, the Jewish nation will not perish.

When the rabbi finished his speech, he approached the five *chalutzim*, blessed each of them and kissed them, and only then were the sobbing parents convinced that their children have become national heroes. They stopped crying and their faces began to glow.

*

[Page 229]

The Jewish population of Svir did not sleep that night; next morning all escorted the 5 heroes to the bridge. When they began their journey it started to rain, but all remained standing and sang the Jewish national anthem *Hatikva* [The hope].

I am sure that each and every one of the persons who was blessed to be on that morning on the bridge will remember these wonderful moments all his or her life. Even the Vilna newspapers found it necessary to print articles about the five Svir *Chalutzim*. The Vilna Jewish daily "*Die Zeit*" had a special report, which brought all the details about the farewell event, and special admiration was expressed for the rabbi and his speech. Since that speech, the rabbi became the darling of the Svir Jewish youth, although most of them were not religious persons.

In Svir, more and more young people joined the pioneer movement, and emigrant groups from Svir left for Eretz Israel frequently.

Among the people who left were Shlomo Chayat and Bat-Sheva Jaffe and Chana Rabinowitz and Ethel Dobkin – and the number of former Svirer in Eretz Israel increased month by month. However, as the years passed, the journey became more and more difficult, and the early trips seemed like child play compared to the latter. We would remember with envy the times when one could reach Eretz Israel in one week. The Aliya became illegal, the trip was challenging and life was in danger. However, the flow of Aliya continued.

In 1939, shortly before the War broke out, six Svir *Chalutzim* – Oizer Miller, Berl Yoel, Herzl Weiner, Feivel Blyacher, Rachel Mechnowitz and Beile Blyacher – started the dangerous journey. They traveled legally up to the Romanian port of

[Page 230]

Constanþa, and there they boarded a ship to Panama, as "tourists." Eight hundred passengers were on board, and on the 4th day they arrived at the shores of Eretz Israel. But British ships guarded the shores and they were forced to sail on. They remained several weeks at sea, until the food ran out, and drinking water was rationed, a small glass a day. Medications were lacking as well. To add to their misfortune, they encountered another ship full of illegal immigrants, which had been 4 months at sea, and they took on board all the passengers. They were now 1,400 persons, many of them exhausted and sick. They tried most of the Mediterranean ports – nowhere were they allowed to disembark. In despair, after 5 weeks of wandering, they decided to sail toward the Eretz Israel shores, even at the risk of being captured. Indeed, as they approached the shore, the British navy ships opened fire. Two of the immigrants were killed and many were wounded. The captain and his crew left the ship and they fled in one of the boats. Finally the Jewish passengers took control of their ship and on Friday evening they reached Tel Aviv. It was a dark night and the people on board immediately began to leave for the shore. However, the British discovered them and those who did not manage to escape in the darkness were arrested and sent to the Sarafand military base, near Rishon LeZion. They remained there a long time, and were released only after great efforts. Many other Svir pioneer immigrants had to undergo the same ordeal before they could finally settle in Eretz Israel.

The Svir "family" in the country increased year by year. After the war, very few Jews remained in Svir. Most of the survivors came to Eretz Israel and only several

[Page 231]

Yosef and David Matzkewitch z"l from Kiryat-Chaim

families traveled from Germany to America. Now there are over 100 Svir families in Israel. They live in Kfar Saba, Tel Aviv, Kiryat Chaim near Haifa, Tel Mond, Jerusalem, Petach Tikva, Ekron near Rehovot and in the kibbutzim Sede Nachum and Ramat Rachel. Almost all of the Svirer in Israel are hard working people and make an honest living.

As time went on, the Svir families in Israel suffered heavy losses as well.

Shlomo Chayat died of a heart attack in Kfar Saba. He was a diligent worker and a conscientious pioneer, and was devoted, body and soul, to the rebuilding of Israel.

Bat-Sheva Jaffe-Ratner from Tel Aviv died of pneumonia. Every immigrant who came from Svir had an address to go to, and it was always Bat-Sheva's address. She welcomed the newcomers and shared her bread with them like a loving sister.

[Page 232]

She lived in a one-room apartment with her husband and child, but her door was open and there was always room for another Svirer to spend the night. With her passing the Svirer lost a true and devoted friend.

In Kibbutz Tel-Yosef, death took away the young Feigele, Reznik's youngest daughter.

In Kfar Saba, Binyamin Kamin died at the age of 44, leaving a wife and four small children. He was a good friend to all Svirer.

Also in Kfar Saba, Chanan Gendel died of heart disease. He was generally a healthy man, but he could not overcome the grief at the terrible death of his son. In Chanan's home the door was always open and he was loved by all Svirer in Israel.

Chana Rabinowitz, Bendel's daughter, died in Jerusalem. She was a hard-working and dedicated lady.

And finally we remember the Svirer who have shed their blood in the war for the independence of the State of Israel, and among the hundreds of Jewish heroes we shall mention them here:

Zev Gendel son of Chanan, who gave his life to save the life of a wounded soldier.

Seadia Grager, Yakov Grager's only son, fell on the battle fields near the Syrian border.

And the two brothers Yosef and David, sons of Zelda Matzkewitch of Kiryat Chaim, who fell both in the same battle, in the attempt to open the road to Kibbutz Yechi'am.

Two other Svirer were seriously wounded in the War of Independence: In May 1948 Baruch Gershowitz lost a leg. He was a driver and on that day he was taking

[Page 233]

food to the soldiers fighting in South-Jerusalem. The Arabs attacked the vehicles with machine-guns and Baruch was hit.

Chanan Weiner, one of the well-known Svir *chalutzim*, a member of the kibbutz Ramat-Rachel, was even more seriously wounded. He was hit in his back and the lower part of his body became paralyzed.

Zev Gendel z"l from Kfar-Saba

This is, in short, the description of the lives of the Svir immigrants in the Land of Israel. For most of them the country was not a land of milk and honey, but of sweat and blood. However, every one of them has managed to build a life and see

[Page 234]

Seadia Grager z"l from Kfar-Saba

happiness, and raise a generation of smart, beautiful and lovable children, named mostly after their dead fathers and mothers. It is interesting – and gratifying – to see that all the children are eager to learn about Svir, the birth town of their parents, and they listen with interest and attention to the stories about the remote little town of Svir.

The Svir tribe living in Israel continues the long chain of generations of the old home and maintains the tradition of friendship, brotherhood and togetherness.

Svirer remain Svirer, wherever they are.

Finally, I shall mention with pleasure and pride the association of all Svir former residents, which carries the Hebrew name *Irgun Yotz'ei Svir Bimedinat Israel* [the Organization of the former Svir Residents in the State of Israel].

[Page 235]

The leader of our association is Dov (Berl) Yoel, Gitel's oldest son, who is working in the offices of the Tel Aviv Municipality. He is devoting all his free time to the Organization and its Free-of-Interest Loan Fund. Just as his mother Gitel, he is involved with all his heart and soul in the good work. His aim is always to help others, exploring all the possibilities. It is simply impossible to imagine the existence of the Svirer association and the loan fund without his help and his energy.

Berl Yoel was one of the first Svirer who realized the meaning and the importance of publishing a special Yizkor Book for our town. Together with him, the members who are contributing time and effort to the work of the organization, the loan-fund and the Yizkor book are Heshel Miller, Gershon Yoel, Shmuel Dobkin, Herzl Weiner, Yosef Desyatnik, Sara Tzach and others. Only thanks to their untiring work and unlimited creativity, thanks to their utmost devotion and enthusiasm, have the Svirer been able to create a literary monument in the form of this book, to serve as a historic remembrance of their nearest and dearest, all those who exist no more.

In the name of all Svirer over the world we sent them a heartfelt thank-you. They have earned it honestly.

[Page 236]

A memorial prayer for former residents of Svir

IDF soldiers who fell in the War of Independence (1948)

Translated by Yocheved Klausner

GENDL	Zeev	son of Chanan & Bila	Kfar Saba
GRAGER	Se'adya	son of Yakov & Chaia Esther	Kfar Saba
MATZKEVITS	David Yosef	sons of Zelda & Yehoshua Leib	Kiryat Chaim

Those who Died in Israel

GENDL	Khone	son of Zeev	Kfar Saba
KHAZAN	Yitskhak Mordekhay		Kiryat Khayim
KHAZAN	Pinkhas	son of Yitskhak Mordekhay	Haifa
CHAYAT	Shlomo	son of Ruven	Kfar Saba
YAFE-RATNER	Bat-Sheva	daughter of David Ber	Tel Aviv
KARMEL	Ida	daughter of Fayve	Tel Aviv
SVIRSKI	Shoshe		Kfar Saba
Tsadok the Shochet			Jerusalem
KURITSKI	Baruch		Petakh Tikva

KAMIN	Binyamin	son of Michael	Kfar Saba
RABINOVITZ	Chana	daughter of Bendet	Tel Aviv
RESNIK	Feygele	daughter of Kofman	Kibutz Tel Yosef
RESNIK-KRUPSKI	Freidl	son of Chaim Yakov	Kiryat Chayim
SHWARTSGAR	Moshe Aron		Jerusalem
SHWARTZGAR	Shoshe		Jerusalem

May their memories be eternally blessed

May their souls be bound in the bond of the living

[Page 237]

List of the Svirer Jews in the Land of Israel

Translated by Yocheved Klausner

Family name(s)	First name(s)	Father's name	Residence
AIZIKOWITZ	Zev	Shlomo-Hirshel	Ramat Gan
AIZIKOWITZ-SVIRSKY	Beile	Shlomo-Hirshel	Givatayim
BABIS	Lea		Tel Aviv
BLACHER	Shmuel	Yehuda	Kfar Azar
BLACHER	Shraga	Yehuda	Kibbutz Bet Hashita
BLEKHER-SHMUSHKOVITZ	Beile	Yitzhak	Tel Aviv
BLEKHER	Bat Sheva	Yitzhak	Tel Aviv
BLEKHER	Yehuda	Yitzhak	Sedema
BLEKHER	Shlomo Kalman	Yehuda Velvl	Jerusalem
BENSMAN	Chaim	Avraham	Afula
GABAY	Elimelekh	Pesach	Rishpon
GORVITZ-MULLER	Pesl	Mendel David	Kfar Saba
GITLIN-GRAGER	Sima	Meir	Kfar Saba
GITLIN	Aharon	Meir	Kfar Baruch

Family name(s)	First name(s)	Father's name	Residence
GERSHOVITZ-GERSHUNI	Baruch	Israel	Jerusalem
GRAGER	Yakov	Eliahu-Chaim	Kfar Saba
GRAGER	Shlomo	Eliahu-Chaim	Kfar Saba
GRAGER-DESYATNIK	Sara Reizl	Eliahu-Chaim	Kfar Saba
GRINBERG-KOTLOVSKI	Gitl		Bet Yehoshua
DOBKIN	Shmuel	Eliahu-Avraham	Tel Aviv
DOBKIN-ZUCHOVITZKI	Ethel	Eliahu-Avraham	Jerusalem
DOBKIN-POLLACK	Tzivie	Eliahu-Avraham	Magdiel
DOBKIN-KURLANDER	Hinde	Eliahu-Avraham	Kfar Saba
DAVIDMAN-HAYISREELI	Risie		Tel Aviv
DESYATNIK-GRAGER	Ite	Efraim	Kfar Saba
DESYATNIK	Yosef	Efraim	Kfar Saba
DRUTZ-SVIRONI	Dr. Chanoch	Zev	Kfar Saba
WEINER-KARMI	Meir	Shmerl	Kibbutz Ramat Rachel
WEINER	Herzl	Yakov-Liber	Kibbutz Sede Nachum
WEINER	Chanan	Yakov-Liber	Kibbutz Ramat Rachel
WEINSTEIN-YOEL	Mina	Hirshe-Nathan	Kibbutz Sede Nachum

[Page 238]

Family name(s)	First name(s)	Father's name	Residence
WEINSTEIN-MUSIN	Miriam	Hirshe-Nathan	Ramat Hasharon
WERZBELOVSKI	Aizik		Benei Brak
ZALMANSON-MALAKHOVSKI	Sara	Baruch	Tel Aviv
CHADASH-WEINSTOCK	Mina		Tel Chanan
CHADASH	Batia	Aizik	Tel Chanan
CHADASH	Miriam	Aizik	Tel Chanan
CHADASH KATZERGINSKI	Sonia		Petach Tikva
CHAZAN DRABKIN	Shoshana	Yitzhak-Mordechai	Kiryat Chaim
CHAZAN-FRIEDMAN	Raya	Yitzhak-Mordechai	Kiryat Chaim
CHAZAN BONISCHEVITZ -	Tzipora	Yitzhak-Mordechai	Haifa
CHAZAN-SKARAPA	Miriam	Yitzhak-Mordechai	Kiryat Motzkin
CHAYAT	Meir	Feive	Kfar Saba

CHAYAT	Chaim	Reuven	Kfar Hess
YOEL	Dov	Zev	Tel Aviv
YOEL	Gershon	Yechiel	Kfar Saba
YOEL	Dov	Yechiel	Kibutz Sede Nachum
YOEL	Nathan	Yechiel	Kibutz Ramat Rachel
YAFFE	Moshe	Dov Ber	Ramat Gan
YAFFE-GRASS	Shoshana	Dov Ber	Tel Aviv
KATZ	Chloyne		Eyn Vered
KATZ	Chananya		Tel Aviv
KARMEL	Sinai		Tel Aviv
LOBINARSKI-POYER	Chiene	Noah	Tel Aviv
MOSENSOHN-GOLDRING	Ester	R'Naftali David	Petach Tikva
MOSENSOHN		R'Naftali David	Tel Aviv
MECHNOWITZ	Hinde	Shimon Eliahu	Kibutz Einat
MECHNOWITZ – BEN-YAAKOV	Rachel	Shimon Eliahu	Kiryat Chaim
MOLLER	Heshel	Moshe	Kfar Saba
MOLLER	Sheine	Moshe	Kfar Saba
MOLLER	Ozer	Moshe	Kfar Saba
MOLLER	Sheitel	Moshe	Giv'at Ada
MOLLER	Eliahu	Shmuel Mordechai	Kfar Saba
MOLLER	Yechiel	Avraham Yitzhak	Bet Elazari
NACHUMSOHN	Reitze		Kfar Saba
NACHUMSOHN	David		Kfar Saba

[Page 239]

Family name(s)	First name(s)	Father's name	Residence
NACHUMSOHN-NUTKOWITZ			Kfar Saba
NACHUMSOHN-SCHILEWITZ			Kfar Saba
SAKHABENSOHN			Bat-Yam
SVIRSKI-AIZIKOWITZ	Keile	Yakov	Kfar-Saba
SVIRSKI	Moshe	Elyakim	Bet Elazari
SVIRSKI	David	Refael	Kfar Saba
SVIRSKI	David	Zalman	Ra'anana
SVIRSKI	Sara	Zalman	Kibutz Ma'abarot
SVIRSKI	Eliahu	Zalman	Ramat-Gan

Family name(s)	First name(s)	Father's name	Residence
SVIRSKI-CHAYAT	Frieda	Mordechai	Kfar Saba
SVIRSKI-SEGAL	Lea	Mordechai	Kfar Kadima
SPECTOR-LIVYATAN	Chaia	Shmuel Yosef	Tel Aviv
EPSTEIN	Chune	Avraham	Petach Tikva
PATOSHNIK-GENDEL	Beile	Shmuel-Meir	Kfar Saba
PATOSHNIK-SHAPIRA	Batia Ethel	Shmuel-Meir	Kfar Saba
PATOSHNIK-REZNIK	Sara	Shmuel-Meir	Kfar Hess
PAPISKI	Mina	Yitzhak	Kibutz Na'an
FISCHER	Yitzhak	Zalman-Mechl	Tel Aviv
FISCHER	Akiva	Zalman-Mechl	Herzliya
FISCHER-LIVYATAN	Fania		Rishon Lezion
FISCHER-MORAVTCHIK	Chaia	Yitzhak	Tel Aviv
PEKING-PEKAL	Arye	Israel	Haifa
TZACH-CHAYAT	Sara	Bendet-Meir	Kfar Saba
TZACH-GRANER	Pera	Bendet-Meir	Kfar Saba
TZERNATZKI-BRAUN	Nechama	Mordechai	Kiryat Amal
KAPLAN-MATZKEWITZ	Zelde	Hirshe	Kiryat Chaim
KAPLAN-REICHELSOHN	Tzipora		Kibutz Afek
KARASIN	Yosef	Mendel	Bet Elazari
KORITZKI-SHAPIRA	Chaia	Baruch	Petach Tikva
RABINOWITZ-MARGOLIN	Tzipora	Bendet	Jerusalem
RAVITZ-GLATT	Lea	Bere-Yakov	Kfar Ono
RAVITZ-COHEN	Pola	Bere-Yakov	Tel Aviv
RUBIN-SCHUSTER	Feigel(Ester)	Rav [rabbi] Yakov	Jerrusalem

[Page 240]

Family name(s)	First name(s)	Father's name	Residence
REZNIK-IVYAN	Tzila	Koifman	Ramat Gan
REZNIK	Dov	Koifman	Tel Aviv
REZNIK	Ita	Chaim	Tel Aviv
REZNIK	Zalman	Chaim Yakov	Petach Tikva
REZNIK-KROKAW	Chasia	Chaim Yakov	Kiryat Chaim
REZNIK	Yehuda	Shmuel	Ramat Gan

REZNIK-SACHS	Tony	Shmuel	Tel Aviv
REZNIK-PEKLER	Merl	Leib	Ramat Gan
REZNIK	Yitzhak	Avraham	Tel Aviv
REZNIK	Avraham-Yitzhak	Katriel	Petach Tikva
SHAPIRA	Aharon		Kfar Saba
SHAPIRA-TZIPELEWITZ	Nechama	Aharon	Kfar Saba
SHAPIRA	Zvi	Aharon	Kfar Saba
STEIN-SOKOL	Lea	(Soloweitchik)	Kfar Munash
SCHEINOK	Leibe		Tel Aviv
SCHEIKON	Eliyahu	Alter	Jerusalem
SCHNEIDEROWITZ	Sima	Leib	Kibutz Giv'at Chayim

NAME INDEX

A

Abel, 129, 159
Abrahams, 153
Aizikovitz, 129
Aizikowitz, 183
Aizikowitz-Svirsky, 183
Alperovitch, 25
Alperovitz, 3, 14, 27, 28, 29, 30, 31, 32, 41, 45, 46, 56, 75, 129
Alperowitz, 156
Alpert, 30
Alzikowitz-Swirski, 158
Antchelevitz, 129
Antsilevitch, 94, 101
Arbin, 73
Ash, 25, 26, 32
Ayzerovitz, 25
Ayzikov, 25, 92
Ayzikovitch, 41, 147
Ayzikovitz, 97
Ayzikovski, 124
Ayzikson, 149

B

Babis, 183
Bakavitch, 44
Barchanowitz, 158
Barovsky, 129
Bensman, 130, 183
Bentsye The Shoemaker, 73
Ben-Tzvi, 174
Ber, 25, 26
Berger, 130
Berkman, 63, 130, 175, 176
Berson, 25, 124
Bialik, 100, 123, 176
Blacher, 183
Blakher, 103
Blekher, 183
Blekher-Shmushkovitz, 183
Bliakher, 129, 130
Blyacher, 164, 168, 174, 177
Blyakher, 94
Bogdanov, 71, 147, 149, 152, 153
Brash, 101
Breslav, 153
Bromberg, 130, 153
Buck, 153
Bukhhalter, 25
Bushkanetz, 157, 158
Bushkanetz-Zlatayawka, 158
Bushkanyetz, 129

C

Chadash, 157, 184
Chadash-Katzerginski, 184
Chadash-Weinstock, 184
Chaiat, 37, 38, 39, 134
Chaim Yisroel The Tinsmith, 47
Charmatz, 135
Chatzkelevitz, 135
Chayat, 9, 147, 152, 154, 157, 166, 168, 171, 172, 174, 176, 178, 182, 184, 185
Chayat-Jaffe, 157
Chayet, 147, 148, 149, 150
Chazan, 9, 174
Chazan-Bonischevitz, 184
Chazan-Drabkin, 184
Chazan-Friedman, 184
Chazan-Skarapa, 184
Chodesh, 175
Cohen, 154

D

Danishevsky, 132
Davidman-Hayisreeli, 184
Desyatnik, 164, 168, 172, 182, 184
Desyatnik-Grager, 184
Deutch, 152, 153
Dimenstein, 158
Dimenstein-Yoel, 157
Dimentshtein, 132
Dimentshteyn, 66, 67
Dobkin, 3, 5, 33, 57, 84, 94, 100, 132, 160, 164, 168, 172, 176, 182, 184
Dobkin-Kurlander, 184
Dobkin-Pollack, 184
Dobkin-Zuchovitzi, 184
Donishevski, 93, 94

Drapkin, 78
Dreviatzki, 133
Drevitzki, 106
Drevnitski, 105
Drevyatski, 29, 31, 55, 64, 99, 115, 116, 123, 124, 125
Drewiatzki, 157
Drobkin, 53
Droyn, 147
Drutz, 1, 3, 8, 11, 21, 26, 28, 29, 35, 38, 60, 76, 105, 123, 132, 133, 151, 165, 168
Drutz- Svironi, 164
Drutz- Sviruni, 73
Drutz-Svironi, 172, 184
Dubkin, 38
Duvnikirer, 13

E

Ekman, 140
Engel, 140
Engle, 32
Epshtayn, 27
Epshteyn, 31, 94
Epstein, 140, 155, 186

F

Falk, 155
Falstein, 155
Fine, 155, 159
Finn, 155
Fischer, 140, 141, 152, 155, 156, 168, 172, 175, 186
Fischer-Livyatan, 186
Fischer-Moravtchik, 186
Fisher, 3, 25, 26, 29, 30, 35, 41, 54, 74, 76, 85, 86, 104, 110, 119, 121, 124, 148, 149, 172
Friedman, 155
Friedshon, 141

G

Gabay, 47, 110, 125, 183
Gabbai, 130
Gabstein, 153
Gargel, 130, 131
Gelgar, 76, 132
Gelgarn, 124
Gelger, 75
Gendel, 132, 174, 179, 180
Gendl, 47, 182

Gerschovitz, 131
Gershater, 36, 132
Gershovits, 95
Gershovitz, 31, 47
Gershovitz-Gershuni, 184
Gershowitz, 179
Gershowitz-Swirski, 157
Ginsburg, 131
Gitlin, 30, 98, 131, 183
Gitlin-Grager, 183
Glasser, 153
Glezer, 131
Gold, 73, 151, 152, 153, 164
Goldman, 26, 130
Gordon, 25, 32, 57, 60, 64, 153, 158
Gorvitz-Muller, 183
Grabeski, 39
Grager, 119, 124, 179, 181, 182, 184
Grager-Desyatnik, 184
Grass, 153
Gravitz, 132
Greenberg, 149, 152, 153
Grinberg, 132
Grinberg-Kotlovski, 184
Grossman, 132
Gur-Arye, 80
Gurewitz, 164
Guris, 131
Gurvitz, 38, 131

H

Hadash, 134
Hafshtein, 133
Harrison, 1, 153
Hayt, 57
Hazan, 27, 79
Heilpern, 153
Hirshbeyn, 26
Hitler, 3, 78, 91, 101, 122, 123, 147, 162
Hoffman, 153
Horowitz, 153
Hugo, 26

I

Isaksohn, 152, 153
Itzkowitz, 152, 153

J

Jaffe, 157, 176

Jaffe-Ratner, 178
Joel, 3, 7

K

Kaganovitz, 47, 142
Kamin, 27, 28, 47, 65, 94, 142, 159, 174, 179, 183
Kanterowitz, 155
Kaplan, 25, 26, 27, 35, 142, 157, 158
Kaplan-Matzkewitz, 186
Kaplan-Reichelsohn, 186
Karasin, 116, 118, 142, 186
Karmel, 182, 185
Karpilevsky, 142, 143
Katcherginski, 46
Katz, 47, 94, 135, 136, 158, 185
Khadash, 103
Khadesh, 47
Khatskelevitch, 31
Khayt, 26, 47
Khazan, 53, 182
Khetser, 57
Khoury, 147, 148, 149, 150
Kisin, 143
Kissin, 25, 41
Kobrin, 25
Konagovitch, 103
Kopelowitz, 155, 156
Koritzki, 156
Koritzki-Shapira, 186
Kory, 152, 155
Koszlovitz, 143
Kot, 111, 118
Kourie, 164, 167
Koury, 8, 70
Kovarski, 29, 30, 57
Kovorski, 28
Krapivnik, 143
Kreitser, 25
Kuritski, 182
Kuritzk, 152
Kuritzki, 174, 175
Kurkus, 112, 117
Kurnatkes, 13
Kurtski, 52
Kutcher, 173

L

Lavanarsky, 136
Lerner, 154

Levin, 147, 149
Levine, 136, 152, 154
Lieber, 154
Lifshitz, 76
Lobinarski-Poyer, 185

M

Malamyak, 32
Margevitz, 65
Markov, 108
Matzkevits, 182
Matzkewitch, 178, 179
Mechnowitz, 156, 157, 177, 185
Mechnowitz-Ben-Yaakov, 185
Meltsarek, 48
Meltser, 99, 121, 124, 125
Meltzer, 86, 99, 105, 107, 110
Melzer, 154, 156
Mendele, 25, 32, 54
Mestitskin, 30
Metz, 154
Meyer, 29, 55
Mikhl The Watchmaker, 125
Mikhnavitch, 66
Mikhnavits, 111, 114
Mikhnovayets, 118
Mikhnovitch, 101
Mikhnovits, 113, 117
Mikhnovitz, 137
Miller, 3, 4, 19, 23, 25, 26, 27, 29, 30, 31, 48, 49, 51, 54, 55, 56, 57, 63, 64, 93, 95, 103, 124, 137, 152, 154, 164, 168, 172, 174, 175, 177, 182
Millner, 157
Milner, 100, 137
Mindel, 137, 156
Mints, 118
Moliere, 26
Moller, 27, 136, 137, 157, 185
Mosensohn, 185
Mosensohn-Goldring, 185
Mosevzon, 22, 29
Moshe The Painter, 16
Moshe-Leyb The Tailor, 73
Motkin, 100
Motskin, 27
Motzkin, 28, 32
Myadler, 13

N

Nachumsohn, 185
Nachumsohn-Nutkowitz, 185
Nachumsohn-Schilewitz, 185
Nakhum, 3
Napoleon, 6, 13, 80
Nosn, 16, 62
Novirovits, 120

P

Paleika, 91
Papisik, 99
Papiski, 186
Patomkin, 155
Patosh, 155
Patoshnik, 152, 155, 157
Patoshnik-Gendel, 186
Patoshnik-Reznik, 186
Patoshnik-Shapira, 186
Pekel, 80
Peking, 141, 157
Peking-Pekal, 186
Peretz, 32
Pitsilekher, 13
Potashnik, 94, 95, 119, 121, 140, 175

R

Rabinovitch, 31, 41, 43, 44, 101
Rabinovitz, 23, 25, 27, 29, 30, 90, 143, 183
Rabinowitz, 155, 176, 179
Rabinowitz-Alperowitz, 156
Rabinowitz-Margolin, 186
Rabkin, 125
Ravitch, 143, 144
Ravitz-Cohen, 186
Ravitz-Glatt, 186
Raz, 148, 149, 152
Razoler, 159
Renik, 110
Resnick, 25, 26, 27, 29, 30, 32
Resnik, 92, 94, 99, 121, 171, 172, 183
Resnik-Krupski, 183
Reznik, 37, 55, 64, 99, 100, 102, 105, 109, 110, 111, 144, 156, 166, 168, 178, 186, 187
Reznik-Ivyan, 186
Reznik-Krokaw, 186
Reznik-Pekler, 187
Reznik-Sachs, 187
Rogov, 25, 32, 57
Rogozin, 155
Rosee, 155
Rosenfeld, 57
Rozaler, 25
Rubin, 144
Rubin-Schuster, 186
Rudnicki, 35
Rugovin, 34, 36, 37

S

Sakhabensohn, 185
Sakhabenzon, 137
Salav, 77
Salkindson, 61
Salkovski, 112, 119, 120
Scheinok, 187
Schneider, 81, 152, 155
Schneiderowitz, 187
Schpialer, 130
Schreider, 157
Schwartz, 37, 38, 39, 155, 171
Schwarz, 168
Schwarzgar, 168, 173, 174
Seirski, 35
Senders, 154
Shabtay, 152
Shapira, 94, 118, 120, 145, 187
Shapira-Tzipelewitz, 187
Shapire, 110
Shapiro, 122
Shayevitz, 144, 145
Shaykin, 101
Shaykon, 145
Shebsl, 152
Sherman, 155
Sheykon, 155
Shmerkovitz, 145
Shneiderovitz, 145
Shohet, 145
Sholem Aleikhem, 26
Shpiyaler, 13
Shrayer, 30
Shreider, 145
Shulamit, 35, 36, 38
Shulman, 155
Shuster, 145
Shvartsgar, 26
Shvartzgar, 25
Shwartsgar, 183
Shwentzyaner, 13

Sidarisky, 139
Sidarski, 152, 154
Solamyak, 47, 93
Solomiak, 159
Solomiyak, 137
Solomyak, 93, 157
Solow, 152, 154
Solowizik, 35
Sosensky, 137
Sotzkever, 139
Spector, 140
Spector-Livyatan, 186
Spekter, 38
Spektor, 103, 104
Stalin, 34
Stein-Sokol, 187
Stern, 155
Stern-Melzer, 156
Strindberg, 32
Striponsky, 139, 140
Sudarski, 148
Sutzkewer, 38
Svirski, 12, 60, 63, 64, 94, 96, 100, 101, 103, 112, 114, 116, 117, 123, 124, 182, 185
Svirski-Aizikowitz, 185
Svirski-Chayat, 186
Svirski-Segal, 186
Svirsky, 12, 25, 26, 29, 41, 138, 139, 183
Swironi, 1, 3, 6, 8, 47, 91, 111, 173
Swirski, 37, 152, 154, 157, 158, 159
Swirski-Bushkanetz, 158
Swirski-Drewiatzki, 157
Swyer, 154
Syken, 154

T

Tabarisk, 53
Tabarisky, 134, 135
Talayke, 121
Tankeler, 26
Telika, 112
Tinkoff, 152
Tischmann, 154
Treyts, 123
Troyts, 124
Troytsen, 117
Tsadok The Shochet, 182
Tsakh, 31, 99, 105, 118, 125
Tsakh-Grager, 119
Tsernatski, 88

Tsernyavski, 112
Tunkel, 26
Tynkoff, 154
Tzach, 108, 164, 182
Tzach-Chayat, 168, 186
Tzach-Graner, 186
Tzakh, 37, 94, 141
Tzarlansky, 141, 142
Tzernatzki-Braun, 186
Tzirlin, 142

V

Valeyke, 111, 115, 117
Vayler, 25, 26
Vayniger, 32
Vaynshteyn, 94
Velvl The Blacksmith, 72
Vigodski, 34
Viner, 57, 93

W

Weiler, 158
Weiner, 3, 12, 15, 16, 17, 28, 29, 31, 48, 63, 64, 67, 133, 153, 168, 172, 177, 179, 182, 184
Weiner-Karmi, 184
Weinstein, 133, 154
Weinstein-Musin, 184
Weinstein-Yoel, 184
Weishkonsky, 133
Weller, 154
Werzbelovski, 184
Wilkomirsky, 133

Y

Yael, 3
Yafe-Ratner, 182
Yaffe, 25, 26, 110, 121, 135, 164, 168, 172, 185
Yaffe-Grass, 185
Yanisky, 135
Yankelevitz, 135, 157
Yankl The Shoemaker, 73
Yashtsik, 118, 119
Yoel, 38, 60, 61, 62, 63, 64, 65, 92, 104, 135, 156, 162, 164, 168, 172, 175, 177, 182, 185
Yoran, 135
Yudes, 16
Yudl, 25
Yuter, 141

Z

Zalman The Barber-Surgeon, 48
Zalmanson-Malakhovski, 184
Zanaratzky, 133
Zeidel, 133
Zeltser, 94
Zeltzer, 134
Zlatavyanke, 101, 102
Zlatavyavka, 76
Zlatayavka, 72, 76, 156
Zlatayavke, 23, 25, 27, 31, 32, 57, 64, 94, 124, 173
Zlatayavski, 94
Zlatayobke, 8
Zlatayovka, 133
Zlatayovke, 32, 94
Zlataywski, 156
Zygowski, 34

www.ingramcontent.com/pod-product-compliance
Lightning Source LLC
Chambersburg PA
CBHW081420160426
42814CB00039B/211